The Boleyns of Hever Castle

by

Owen Emmerson
Claire Ridgway

The Boleyns of Hever Castle

ISBN-13: 978-84-122325-6-1

Cover Image: Hever Castle, David Cox the Younger, c.1850, Watercolour & Ink Reproduced from the collection of Dr Owen Emmerson.

Cover design and layout: MadeGlobal Publishing

M
MadeGlobal Publishing

For more information on
MadeGlobal Publishing, visit our website:
www.madeglobal.com

Contents

Dedications

To Maurice Forbes-Wood, my lovely grandad, who lives on in our hearts and on the page of this book.

Owen

To Tim, who always has my back and never lets me give up.

Claire

Travel Back in Time to the Boleyns' Home

BEFORE WE begin to explore the complex and colourful lives of the Boleyns of Hever Castle, who called this place 'home' for seventy-seven years, let us introduce you to Hever by way of a tour of the castle. Some of you may have visited this extraordinary surviving property, and others may not. Still, the Hever that we will explore now hasn't been seen since the Boleyns finally left in 1540, so we will journey through Hever Castle as the Boleyn family most likely knew it.

There has been some debate about how much of the Boleyns' house at Hever survives, with attention made to the three significant restoration periods between 1830-1903. While the layout of some chambers has altered, the usage of some rooms changed, and a later veneer of fittings and furnishings added, this is overwhelmingly the same space that the Boleyn family occupied. We are walking in the footsteps of this notorious family, who set the country in a roar and who made Hever endlessly famous. The year is 1513.

First impressions

STANDING ON the ridge of a hill to the southwest, just by Hever's St Peter's Church, Hever Castle stands at the bottom of a basin, just to the south of the river Eden: white, moated, and majestic. This castle is not alone, for many outbuildings surround the castle, and the activities in these many simpler buildings, and the work of its inhabitants, are part of the established mechanisms by which Hever functions. Because the moat feeds from the unpredictable river, it has been known to flood on occasion. But this modest castle is perfect for the Boleyns. Indeed, it sits at the very heart of Thomas Boleyn's world. We are a day's ride to Henry VIII's favoured palace of Greenwich, and the same distance to Dover, from where many voyages for Thomas' diplomatic missions for the king will depart. Hever is a place of safety and privacy for the Boleyns. Thomas's father, William Boleyn, gave his daughter-in-law, Lady Elizabeth Howard, a lifetime stake in Hever Castle as part of her wedding dower. Thomas and Elizabeth are joint owners of Hever, and they have placed their children where they are most accessible.

There are much grander and newer manors in the Boleyns' increasingly impressive portfolio of properties, so the Boleyns do not need to be at Hever: they want and choose to be here. Again, and again later in the 1520s, we find the Boleyns at Hever. Thomas does much business from here, being a diligent steward to his lands and the nearby crown property of Penshurst, of which Thomas is appointed steward. Later, Anne uses Hever as almost a safety valve to take the pressure off her as she negotiates the uncharted and turbulent waters created in the wake of Henry's determination to marry her. Hever is close to Henry's court, private, and somewhere shaded from the heat of scandal and gossip, and Anne's absence drives the king to write steamy love letters to her here. Absence makes Henry's heart grow that much fonder for Anne that he feels compelled to enclose her initials in a heart.

Hever Castle from St Peter's Church by David Cox Jnr, 19th century

There is a long tradition that Thomas and Elizabeth's five children - Thomas, Mary, Anne, George, and Henry - spent their childhood here from 1505. By 1513, two of the Boleyn boys have died. The graves survive today and have been statistically dated to between 1505-35. These lost Boleyn boys likely died in infancy. By 1513, Hever has been a site of much sorrow for Thomas and Elizabeth Boleyn. It is, however, now a flurry of excitement, for Thomas's ability to ingratiate himself with those he is sent to do diplomacy for the king has won his daughters coveted places to finish their education at two European courts. Hever is soon to be a smaller household, for Anne Boleyn is headed to the court of Margaret of Austria in the Low Countries, and soon, her sister Mary will head to the court of France.

With Hever's Church of St Peter behind us, we head down the main road, which takes us far closer to the castle than that which exists today. Hever is open to the traveller's eye. Dismantled in the 1890s, Hever's first line of defence is a guardhouse: a simple two-storey structure from which an alarm could be raised to the main fortress. We pass without challenge, for we are welcome visitors today. As we continue, a vast wooden building stands to our right beyond a large pond that feeds from the outer moat. Hever elegantly emerges from the water of the inner moat to our left-hand side as we approach the castle's keep.

Castle Forecourt

YOU MAY well have seen the actor Richard Burton as Henry VIII riding his horse over the drawbridge and into Hever's courtyard. What you don't see on screen is the wooden ramp the production company installed to facilitate the horse getting down the rather steep steps into the courtyard. In the Boleyns' time, the steps are somewhat shallower, for William Waldorf Astor lowered the ground floor level from 1903 to provide more height to the ground floor chambers. However, the Boleyns don't need to ride into the castle courtyard, for the great Tudor stables are located slightly southwest in front of the castle. This is an impressive two-storey building, with five sleeping chambers above the stables for the groomsmen and a large, vaulted chamber with a crown post roof. On the south face is a beautiful open balcony with stairs leading down. This is a hive of activity when the Boleyns are in residence, as much of their sport here - boar and deer hunting - requires its workers to tend to their horses constantly.

Approaching the castle, we notice the partially stone bridge across the moat, with a wooden drawbridge leading to the keep. The drawbridge can, if necessary, be hauled up at a moment's notice to protect the Boleyn family. Hever has always been a home, but it is far more so now in this period of relative peace and stability. The original medieval defensive mechanisms are still in place and fully functional. Above our heads are beautifully formed machicolations: overhanging protrusions from the roof of the gatehouse through which arrows and heavy detritus could be propelled down. Just as the drawbridge can be pulled up, no less than three wooden portcullises can be dropped down from the chambers above. Lattice gates can be locked behind the first portcullis, and a vast oak door closed in front of the third. If trapped between these portcullises, murder holes can be opened from the keep's central chamber, and arrows fired down them. Even in a time of peace, Hever is prepared to be deadly to those who arrive without an invitation.

Sketch of Hever's gatehouse, 19th century
NEXT PAGE: Hever Castle with the Tudor stables, 19th century

Castle Courtyard

WE CAN smell the house before we see it. When the Boleyn family is at home, ten fireplaces can be burning during the colder months, and the courtyard occasionally blusters with smoke when the wind changes. Before us are a functioning courtyard and a beautifully half-timbered manor house. There are two floors in this house and five doors for us to choose to enter from the courtyard. We shall explore beyond all of them.

If we step down two steps into the courtyard, there is a criss-cross of paths to the main doors of the house, for this is a functioning courtyard. The path between the gatehouse and the main doors is offset slightly as the keep itself has an offset gateway, being positioned to the east of the structure. This is to afford two additional chambers besides the space required on the middle floor to raise the portcullises and the mechanisms to raise them on the upper floor. Turning back to look at the inner south face of the keep, we see two doors on either side of the gatehouse. To the left is a vice staircase that travels the full height of the imposing structure. To the right is a door into the guardhouse. We can still see the now bricked up remnants of this door today.

Turning clockwise, we see another unfamiliar door between the bays of the west elevation of the house. This doorway leads to the chatelaine's offices and Thomas Boleyn's study. This is the business floor of the household. Much of the light to these rooms is drawn from the castle's centre via the bay window into the courtyard. To the north of this area is a staircase, now long gone, which leads to the family apartments.

The next door, opposite the gatehouse, is the family door, and it has a small porch that leads to the screens passage and the great hall to the left-hand side. This is the door through which every generation of the Boleyn family that has resided here has passed. It is also the door by which their friends, family and visitors enter. Some particularly important heads have travelled under the stunning medieval arch to the screens passage, which remains intact today thanks to the protection of the porch. We will travel through the fifth and final door and explore domestic Hever before visiting the family apartments.

Reconstruction of Hever's gatehouse in the Boleyns' era, with three portcullises and porch.
NEXT PAGE: Reconstruction of the Boleyns' great kitchens.

Domestic Hever

SEVERAL SMELLS hit us as we walk through the door on the east elevation: dairy, raw hung meat, and smoke from the nearby kitchens. This is the servants' side of the household, and it is a vastly different realm from the comfy family home. The buttery, to our right, is one of the coolest parts of the household as the sun only touches its walls briefly as it rises. Here, milk from the Hever estate is prepared, and cream turned to butter. To the left of the buttery, the larder contains the produce for the house and is also kept cool with the exterior thick stone walls starved of sunlight.

Travelling left, we enter the great kitchens. There are two roaring fireplaces here against the east elevation, and these are the very heart of the kitchen. The chimney stack that feeds the boisterous fireplaces will later collapse in the nineteenth century when this space stopped being used as the main kitchens for the house. The kitchens are in their heyday during the Boleyns' tenure, and it is a site of significant labour when running at its full capacity. This is very much a male-dominated space, and the roof is double height to help with the often-overpowering heat of the fireplaces with large joints roasting for the Boleyns' table. We could venture through a small service passageway on the west wall of the kitchens, which leads to the more public areas of the family home. We could also alight a staircase that the Boleyns have added with a tower in brick on the east curtain wall. This would take us to a large dormitory where the principal servants bed down. Instead, we are going to retrace our steps and return briefly to the courtyard.

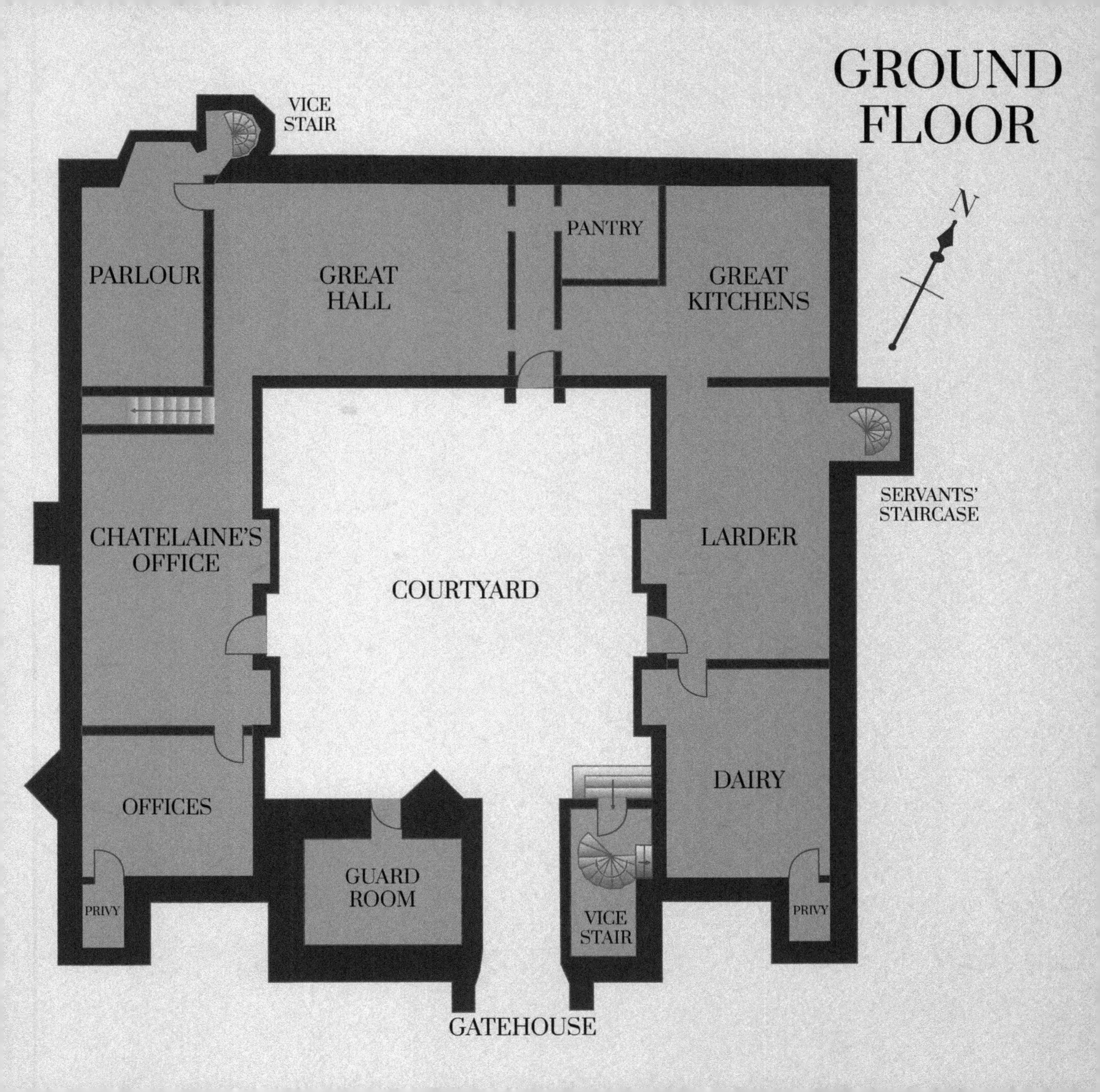
GROUND
FLOOR
VICE
STAIR
N
PARLOUR
GREAT
HALL
PANTRY
GREAT
KITCHENS
SERVANTS'
STAIRCASE
CHATELAINE'S
OFFICE
COURTYARD
LARDER
DAIRY
OFFICES
GUARD
ROOM
PRIVY
VICE
STAIR
PRIVY
GATEHOUSE

The Centrepiece

AS WE approach the family entrance, with its modest little porch and arched doorway, we step directly into the screens passage, the screen being located to the east end of the great hall. Turning left, we enter this major room of the Boleyns' house. This space was once greater still, as it once stretched fully to the west curtain wall, but it retains its original crown post roof. The Boleyns have made the arrangements of this room much more comfortable. A small chamber has been added to the west of the great hall, making the space more compact. Gone is the original central hearth and the open smoke hole in the roof. In its place, a side fireplace has been added, which heats the chamber more efficiently. This is a room with many functions, and not least eating. Much revelry has been enjoyed in this space. The hearth here has consumed many festive Yule logs and the various fine tapestries, which glitter by the naked flame, hold strong the scent of smoky and celebratory evenings.

For all the room's splendour, the Boleyns only eat here when celebrating important feast days and entertaining parties of guests. The occupants of the outbuildings and their estate tenants will also join them at Christmas and will be gifted food to take home. Their most important guests dine with the family on the dais: the raised platform at the west end of the hall, which is lit by a newly cut window. Below this large window are the aumbries of the great hall, where plate can be stored and displayed. When alone, the Boleyns dine "en famille" in their private great chamber, and their closest friends can dine with them there too. The great hall is more generally a public space where the household can dine and where the more junior staff can bed down by the embers of the fire. What makes the room even more public is a small peephole window situated high on the west screen. This is where the family can, should they wish, observe the activities of their servants from their private chambers above. Decorating this screen, which divides the great hall, are carved, green men. To the north of the screen is a door, which we pass through.

Reconstruction of the Boleyns' great hall

The Boleyns' Inner Sanctum

YOU ARE a valued guest if you have made it this far into the Boleyns' privy apartments. There is no confusing this wing of the household with the domestic spaces we visited so far. The Boleyns created this small, tapestried room from the west end of the original great hall, and it is much more comfortable, and warmer too. This new room, which the Boleyn women would chiefly use, gains all the benefit of having the old large oriel window, which once provided light to the head of the household on the dais of the great hall. This room gets all the afternoon sunlight, and the rippling moat creates stunning and often mesmerising silhouettes on the ceiling before the window. A fireplace has also been added, which is a necessity in the frozen months, and it shares a chimney with the chamber above.

This room is where a very young Anne and Mary have learnt numerous stitches from their governess, Mrs Orchard, their mother, Lady Elizabeth Howard, and their grandmother, Lady Margaret Butler. Here, the women of the household talk – or parlay (hence 'parlour') – and complete the blackwork for their smocks and the shirts for the men of the household. This isn't considered labour for women of the Boleyns' status, for all its effort. One wall-hanging is pulled back in the northeast corner, and an open door leads to a stone vice staircase.

Having climbed the staircase, which spirals in an anti-clockwise fashion, we enter a moderately sized antechamber. We are now in the Boleyns' solar, a suite of family rooms that is undoubtedly the most comfortable and private area at Hever. Just as the great hall is a room of many functions, so too is this space. The oriel window continues up to this space. This chamber, with its small low window, allows us to gaze down into the great hall.

The Boleyns' parlour today.
NEXT PAGE: Reconstruction of the Boleyns' great chamber.

The great chamber is the very heart of the Boleyns' family home here at Hever, and this is where we find the finest furniture and furnishings. Carpets have been imported from the Continent, and elegantly carved mahogany furniture can be found throughout. The chamber has painted panelling full of emblems, which meet with fine tapestries and arras hanging on the walls. In modern terms, this is their multifunctional living room. In previous years, it has also functioned as the nursery and schoolroom to the Boleyn children, and they bedded down together here too. Many conversations about the arts, religion, and politics have been and will be had in this most private space. Hever isn't modern or massive, but it is discrete. Forbidden subjects, such as religious reform, will be spoken more easily in these trustworthy walls. Unthinkable achievements, such as wearing the crown of England, will later be discussed here too.

The best bedchamber lies beyond a door to the west of the great chamber. This bedchamber has a sizeable fireplace on the west curtain wall and a luxurious bed with curtains and a tester roof. Its walls are similarly hung with precious textiles. This is the chamber that Thomas and Elizabeth occupy when they are together at Hever. A small doorway to the southwest leads to a garderobe, which has been built into the castle's west tower. Another door in the southeast corner leads into the original castle keep, with a staircase to the righthand side and a door ahead.

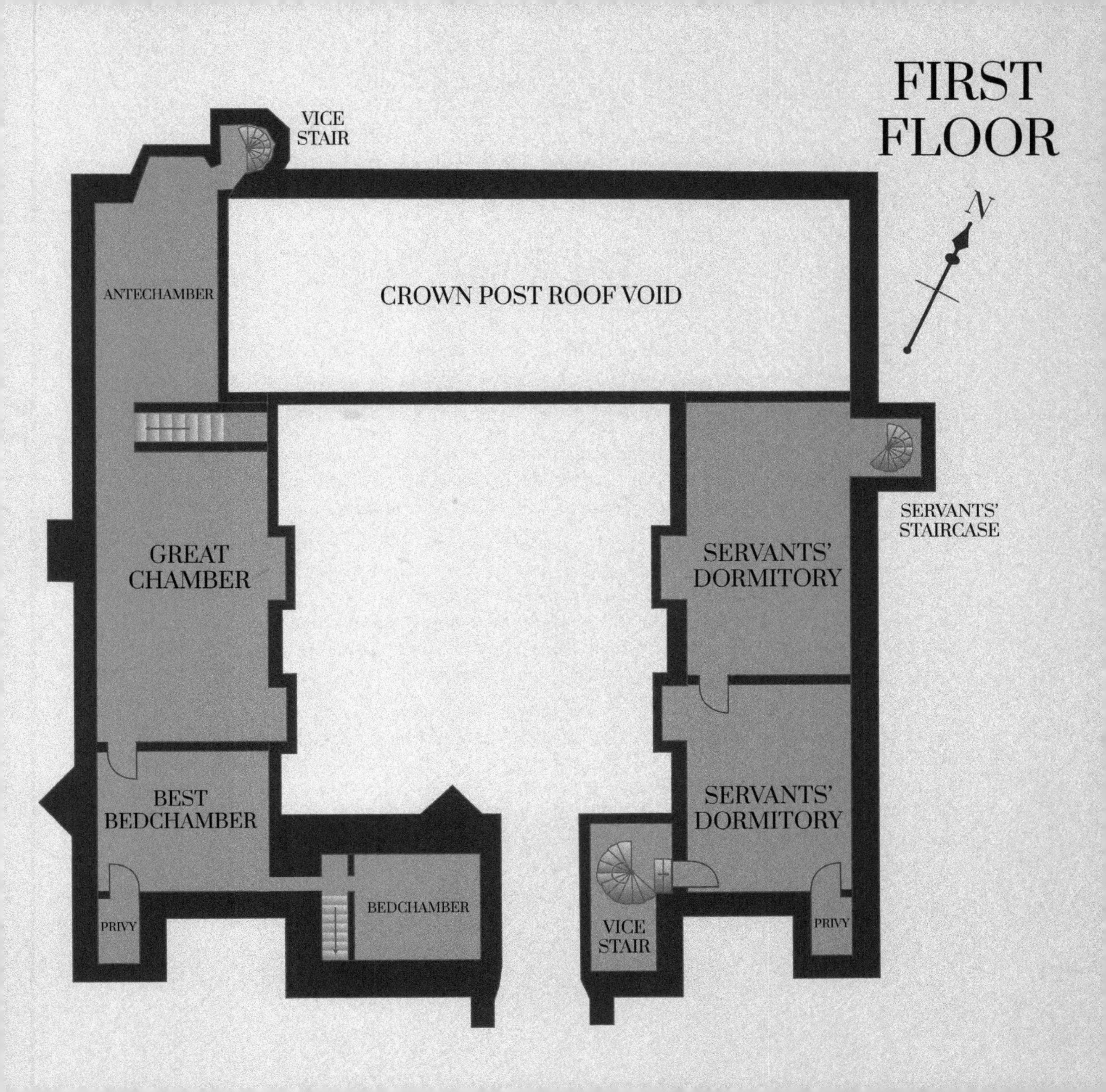
FIRST FLOOR
N
VICE STAIR
ANTECHAMBER
CROWN POST ROOF VOID
GREAT CHAMBER
SERVANTS' STAIRCASE
SERVANTS' DORMITORY
BEST BEDCHAMBER
SERVANTS' DORMITORY
BEDCHAMBER
PRIVY
VICE STAIR
PRIVY

The Keep

THE OFFSET keep allows for three upper chambers in the castle's keep, with the guardhouse below making a fourth. The door ahead takes us to another antechamber which can also, if necessary, operate as another bedchamber. The fireplace here feeds all three upper chambers, and it makes for a comfortable place to retire and catch up on correspondence. It may well be in this space that Thomas Boleyn reads the letter Anne writes him a year later in 1514 from the court of Archduchess Margaret of Austria. It may also be the room where Anne Boleyn reads and replies to King Henry VIII's letters.

Walking up that steep set of stairs we just now encountered, lit by a small window to our right, we enter another larger chamber. This space has been partitioned off, for beyond its east wall are apertures for the three portcullises to ascend. Again, this is a comfortable chamber with ample room for accommodation, and the need to lower the portcullises beyond is so infrequent now that they are a silent presence in the space beyond. The fireplace makes this a readily warm space, and the south-facing window provides good light in the day.

A passageway to the east leads us past the portcullis channel, which is panelled, and to the vice staircase of the castle's keep. Heading up a flight of stairs, curved clockwise, we enter another passageway. To our right is a large winch for the inner portcullis, and beyond the discrete door in the panelling to our left are another winch and a smaller trestle winch in the centre for the middle portcullis. Carrying on along the passage, we find a twin chamber to the one below, again borrowing the chimney for its fireplace.

THIRD FLOOR KEEP

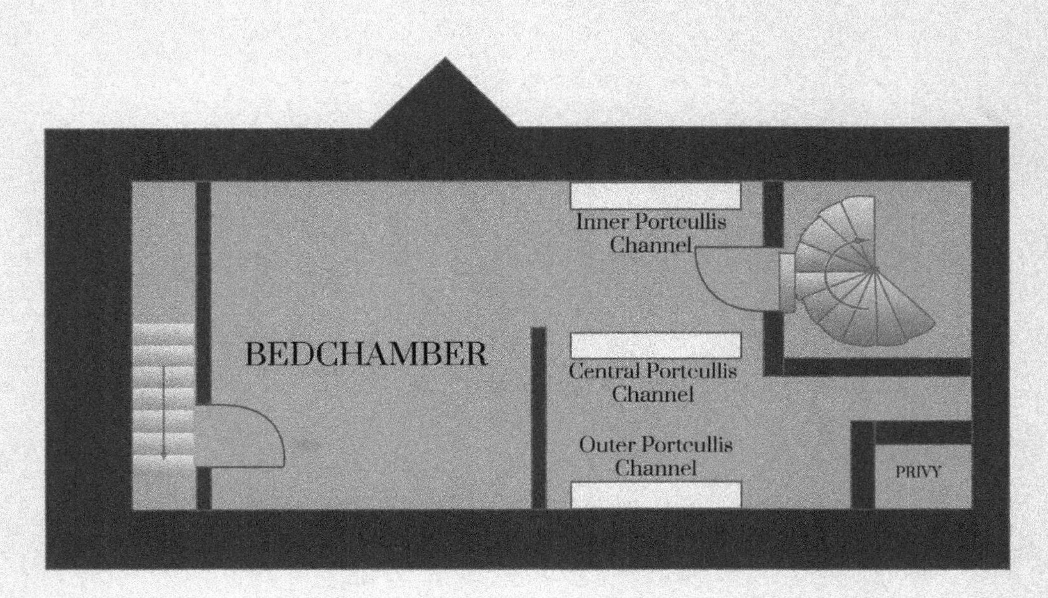

FOURTH FLOOR KEEP

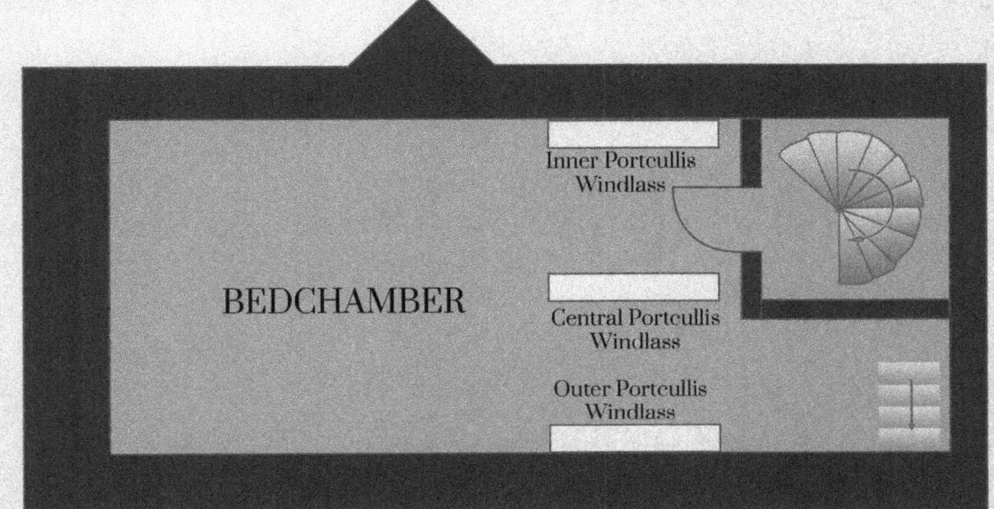

STAIRS TO ROOF

The Roof

RETURNING ONCE again to the passageway, we enter through the discrete door into the space housing the two previously hidden winches. There is also a door on the east face of the chamber, through which we enter. It leads to another steep stone staircase, with a dummy gun port to the right, from which a small window to the left borrows some light for the winch chamber. Carrying up the staircase, we exit through a door to the left, which takes us to the keep's roof. This is where archers can fire through the castle crenels or down the machicolations and then hide behind the merlons. The square chimney stack sits to the north of the roof. Now in more peaceful times, it has provided much entertainment for the Boleyn children in the past years.

The views from the roof are breathtaking. We can see the River Eden snake past the castle to the north and the Church of St Peter to the southeast, with the great Tudor stables in between. This is a thickly wooded part of the Kentish Weald, and the great oak trees will provide not only comfort by way of heat, but later in the Tudor era, will provide significant profit by way of the iron industry and their use to fuel the furnaces. This is a vastly different landscape to the one seen today, with marshland to the east. It is a haven.

Hever is by no means the Boleyns' only property. Indeed, Thomas Boleyn has inherited and amassed a good number of properties, some of which are let out for income and others occupied when the family is in Norfolk or London. Hever is, however, a place that the Boleyns will return to again and again in the late 1520s, when the King of England turns his attention to Anne Boleyn. Far more extravagant furnishings will occupy these chambers in the coming years when Anne achieves the unthinkable, and Thomas Boleyn assumes the role of King Henry's father-in-law. Many tears will be shed within these walls when both Anne and her younger brother George are suddenly and brutally killed barely a thousand days later. The whistle of the French sword upon Tower Green on 19th May 1536 will sound the death knell of the Boleyns of Hever.

After seventy-seven years of family ownership, and after both Elizabeth and Thomas's deaths, the castle is sold by indenture to the Crown, and Henry takes possession of the castle his now-deceased second queen called 'home'. Hever Castle was, for a time, the jewel in the Boleyns' crown as it signified their exceptional rise to nobility. This is the story of the rise of a remarkable family who, over five generations, rose from petty crime to a castle, from Hever to the throne of England.

Aerial photo of Hever Castle today

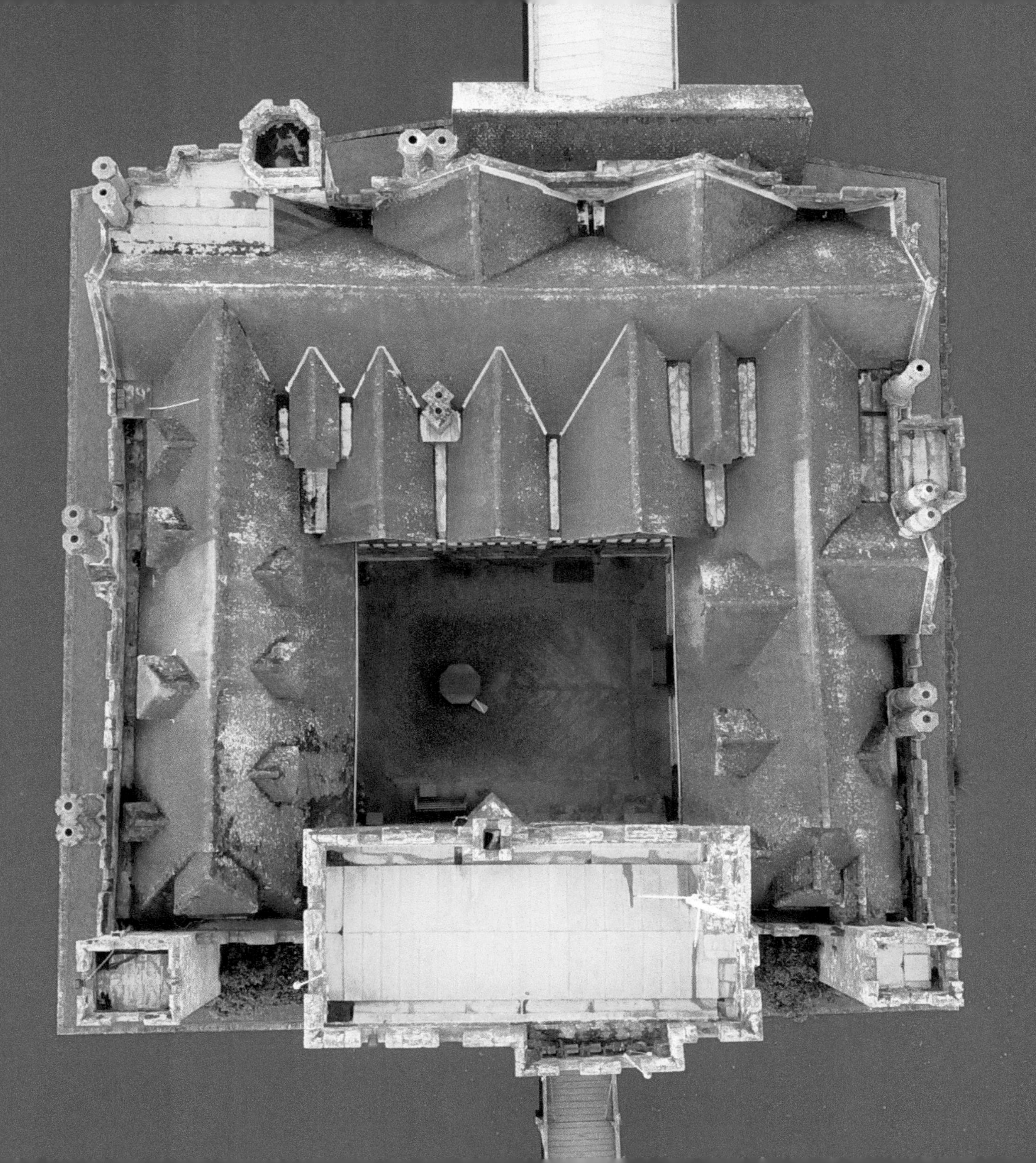

The Boleyns of Hever Castle
(1462-1505)

IN MODERN popular culture, Anne Boleyn's story is portrayed as one of rags-to-riches, and Hever, the Boleyn's little family castle, is used to emphasise her extraordinary rise. This version of Anne is the daughter of a ruthless Kentish knight, willing to pawn his daughters for power. Because of her families' merciless scheming, Anne is propelled from her modest moated manor house to the magnificence of the palaces of King Henry VIII. The Boleyns shown on film and television are grasping, ruthless and thoroughly unlikeable. Their dramatic end is often viewed as 'just desserts' for daring to aim too high.[1]

This story is so familiar in the public consciousness that it seems implausible that the Boleyns revealed to us in the archives are far more complex and interesting than this tired trope suggests.[2] The Boleyns were most certainly ambitious, but their fortune and extraordinary rise had taken place long before Henry VIII decided to pursue the dazzling Anne Boleyn. As the historian Lauren Mackay has argued in her compelling revision of this stereotyping of the Boleyns, it was the family's rise in the fifteenth century that enabled the Boleyns to flourish in the early sixteenth century. The first Boleyns of Hever Castle achieved their wealth and status, rather than being born into it, as Anne Boleyn was.[3]

Our story begins not at Hever Castle, nor in Kent, but in the county of Norfolk where all the Boleyns of Hever Castle were likely born. It is believed that the family had their roots in France and may have descended from the Counts of Boulogne, who came over to England with the Norman invasion in the eleventh century and who settled first in Somerset and Surrey.[4] There are family trees that trace the Boleyn family back to Eustace I, Count of Boulogne (d.1049), who was descended from Baldwin II, Count of Flanders, and Ælfthryth, daughter of Alfred the Great. However, it is impossible to say whether these family trees are accurate. By the mid-thirteenth

---

1 The popular novel *The Other Boleyn Girl* (2003) by Philippa Gregory is a good example of this trope, carried on by the celebrated Booker-prize winning writer Hilary Mantel in the *Wolf Hall* trilogy.

2 For a detailed analysis of the reputation of the Boleyns in popular culture, see Bordo (2013) and Russo (2020)

3 Mackay (2018), p. 8.

4 Bullen (2008); Powlett (1889), Volume 1, pp.27–29; Parsons (1935) pp. 386-407.

century, the 'de Boleyne' or 'de Boulogne' family had settled in Norfolk in a small parish called Salle.

Around the time that John de Cobham of Devonshire, a wealthy Sussex landowner and tax collector, was granted a licence to crenellate his Kentish manor of Hever by King Richard II in 1383, Geoffrey Boleyn Senior was born in Salle. Hever and Salle were remarkably similar in population size, but the social standing of the Boleyns a generation before they would own Hever was vastly below that of the builder of Hever Castle. For many years it was believed that Hever Castle had been built in 1271; however, John Goodall, Anthony Emery, John Newman and Nikolaus Pevsner have all forcefully argued that stylistically, the Hever Castle which stands today was built later, in 1383, in the wake of a period of considerable social unrest.[5]

The Peasants' Revolt of 1381, when the Kentish-born Wat Tyler marched on King Richard II, was emblematic of the social unrest which ripped through England like the 'Great Storm' of that year. Plague, rising taxation to fund war with France, and protest about serfdom dramatically came to a head with the rebels storming the Tower of London and beheading the king's right-hand man. The brutal beheading of Archbishop of Canterbury and Lord Chancellor Simon Sudbury no doubt underpinned the reason for John de Cobham wanting to fortify his principal property of Hever. This was a castle designed to protect the occupants from internal strife as much as any threat of invasion. Before the Boleyns changed its name to 'Hever Castle', it bore the name of 'Hever Cobham' in recognition of the owner who built high the sandstone walls around the manor house.

Geoffrey Boleyn Senior's life in Salle was markedly different from that of Hever Castle's builder. He was born as a worker of the land, not an owner of it. He was employed as a tenant farmer, and there is also evidence that he was involved in the wool trade. Much of our information on Geoffrey's life is from the courts and shows him to be on the fringes of the law, being regularly involved in petty crimes.[6] Many of these incidents centralise around his involvement with the

---

5 See Goodall (2011), pp. 233, 261; Goodhall (2014), pp. 46-50; Emery (2006), Vol III, pp. 355-6 and Newman & Pevsner (2012), p. 311.

6 For a thorough analysis of the career of Geoffrey Boleyn Senior, see Mackay (2018), pp. 10-11.

Sir Geoffrey Bullen
1462

building and repair of Salle Church, such as illegally storing timbers.[7] It appears that he and his father, Thomas Bulleyn of Salle, were involved in building the parish church, even if Geoffrey Senior's methods were on the edge of what was considered legal and proper. Later, he was also found to be extending the parameters of the modest land he acquired by over ploughing.[8] Geoffrey Boleyn Senior spent his life 'getting by'. His son, also called Geoffrey Boleyn, would radically change the fortunes of the Boleyn family.

Geoffrey Boleyn was the first of the Boleyns to amass enough of a fortune to own Hever Castle. He was born around 1405[9] and was the son of Geoffrey Boleyn Senior (d. 1440) and his wife, Alice, who were both buried in the church at Salle.[10] Geoffrey Boleyn is the one who brought the Boleyn family to prominence through his activities in London, and it is Sir John Fastolf, a previous owner of Hever Castle, who is partly responsible for Geoffrey's success. Fastolf favoured the young Geoffrey and took him to London, where he helped him get established.[11] In June 1428, Geoffrey was "admitted into the freedom of the City in the Art of Hatter", and in February 1435, he was admitted as a mercer.[12]

This was a time of increasing opportunity as wealth and power were incredibly attainable by those with inherited status and those with acumen and skill. Historian Eric Ives draws our attention to the fact that William de la Pole, whose great-grandfather had been a merchant in Hull, had been created Duke of Suffolk in 1448. Geoffrey Boleyn was one of the new men who would rise to power, and he solidified his successes with an advantageous marriage into the nobility, taking Anne Hoo, daughter of nobleman Sir Thomas Hoo, the future Lord Hoo and Hastings, as his second wife – his first wife, Dionise, having died. As William Dean states,

---

7 Cited in Parsons (1935), pp. 389-90.

8 *Ibid*, pp. 390-91.

9 Dean (1987), p. 5. Dean notes that Gavin Astor in "The Bullens of Hever" states that Geoffrey was born in 1407.

10 Blomefield (1808), Vol VIII, p. 275.

11 Dean (1987), p. 6.

12 Calendar of Letter-Books of the City of London: K, Henry VI, p. 201

The arms of Geoffrey Boleyn in Hever Castle's long gallery

Geoffrey was the "pivotal Boleyn", and his rise in wealth and status would ensure that his surviving male heir, William Boleyn, was a respectable gentleman.[13]

In September 1446, Geoffrey was appointed as a sheriff for London and Middlesex, and in 1449 he was called to Parliament as a member for London. Three years later, he was appointed as an alderman for Castle Baynard in London. In 1451, Geoffrey was able to loan King Henry VI £1,246 13s. 4d. for an expedition to France, on the understanding that it would be paid back in 1453.[14] Then, in 1452, Geoffrey began negotiations with Sir John Fastolf to purchase Blickling Manor in Norfolk, although there was wrangling for a time over the purchase and its conditions.[15] He then set about adding to it and turning it into the ancestral seat of the Boleyn family. Either Geoffrey extended the manor Fastolf sold him, or created an entirely new build, as it was noted that "Syr Geffrey builded a fair house of brike".[16]

Back in London, Geoffrey became master of the Mercers' Company in 1454, and then, in 1457, he was made Lord Mayor of London and knighted. His time as mayor coincided with the civil war now known as the Wars of the Roses, and as mayor, he was tasked with organising a force to keep order in London and being vigilant for any signs of disorder.

Geoffrey served one term as mayor, and in May 1462, on the Pardon Roll, he appeared as "alderman of London, alias merchant, alias tenant of the manors of Lord Saye and Sele, alias late sheriff, alias late mayor, alias tenant of the lands of Sir Thomas Hoo, deceased, alias Geoffrey Boleyn and Anne his wife, da. and coh. of Thomas Hoo, lord Hoo and Hastings."[17] By 1460, he owned the Norfolk manors of Stivekey, Poswick and Little Carbrook, and had also purchased

13 Dean (1987), p. 11.

14 Calendar of Patent Rolls, Henry VI, Volume V, 1446-1452, p. 472.

15 The Paston Letters, Vol II, pp. 277, 279.

16 Toulman Smith ed. (1908), Volume II, p. 9.

17 Wedgewood (1936), p. 91, citing Pardon Roll, 1462, m.19.

The original door to the screens passage, with trefoils on the spandrels

Kemsing and Sele in Kent.[18] Then, in 1462, Geoffrey and his brother Thomas acquired lands in Kent, which included the manor of Hever, of which Geoffrey took ownership.[19]

Perhaps the brothers took a day out to ride to the vast Kentish estate they intended to purchase together. They may have gazed upon the quaint white castle of Hever Cobham, rising from the river-fed moat, and it could have been at this point that Geoffrey earmarked the castle for his own. Indeed, Geoffrey would buy out his brother from the syndicate and take ownership of the manors of Hever.

The story goes that Geoffrey Boleyn cleverly inserted a manor house between the crenellated walls of the earlier Hever Castle. Eric Ives named Geoffrey the builder of the house.[20] However, although it is likely that it was Geoffrey who completed a substantial amount of work on the original medieval great hall, he had only three years in which to complete any desired renovations and therefore did little to change the fundamental structure of the medieval house that survives today. One of the most evocative visual remnants of the original house is the archway to the screens passage, which visitors to Hever Castle can still see.

Geoffrey partitioned off the westernmost bay of the medieval great hall to create a more private reception room or parlour. The screen that facilitated this partition was beautifully decorated by green men - or foliate heads - which can often be found amongst the earliest symbols in Norman buildings and medieval churches and are believed to symbolise fertility. A door was added to the north side of this screen, and a fireplace built to heat this smaller parlour, with a vast oriel window for light. A side fireplace was added to the great hall, which meant that the medieval smoke hole, previously in the centre of the magnificent crown post roof, could be sealed. This made for a far more comfortable room, which had also been made considerably lighter by the addition of three windows on the north wall. This considerably added to the light

---

18 Blomefield (1808), Volume IX, p. 252; Volume VII, pp. 249-50; Dean (1987), p. 10.

19 Catalogue of Ancient Deeds, Volume I, C.137, C. 862; Volume II, C. 1784, C. 2624; Volume VI, C. 5972; Dean (1987), p. 10.

20 Ives (2004), p. 3.

- the hall having previously been lit by those windows situated to the south, facing the castle's courtyard.

Geoffrey didn't have much time to enjoy his new manor, for he died on 17th June 1463 and was buried in the Church of St Laurence, Jewry, London, which was unfortunately destroyed in the Great Fire of 1666. He died a wealthy man, owning manors, lands and tenements in Kent, Middlesex, Norfolk, Surrey, and Sussex. Geoffrey had provided well for his wife and their five children: Alice, who married Sir John Fortescue; Isabel, who married William Cheyney; Anne, who married Sir Henry Heydon of Baconsthorpe; Thomas (born c.1445), who was unmarried; and William (born c.1448). Geoffrey's sons, Thomas and William, were eighteen and fifteen respectively at the time of their father's death, but Thomas died in April 1471 unmarried and childless, and it was William who was granted his patrimony in March 1473 after he had turned 25, inheriting Hever Castle, among other manors.

Sometime before 1475, William married Lady Margaret Butler, daughter and co-heir of Thomas Butler, 7th Earl of Ormond, of Kilkenny Castle, in Ireland. This was the second great marriage into the nobility for the Boleyns. It was a particularly good match for William as the Butlers had a long history of service to the monarch and Margaret's father owned land in Ireland and England. The Butlers suffered a fall in favour in the 1460s due to their Lancastrian allegiance, but their fortunes changed for the better when Henry VII came to the throne in 1485. Ormond was appointed chamberlain to Henry's queen consort, Elizabeth of York, a position in which he also later served Katherine of Aragon.

William Boleyn built a career not in trade, like his father, but at court. William was made a Knight of the Bath during Richard III's coronation celebrations in 1483 and served as a commissioner of the peace in Norfolk in Richard's reign. In 1483, John Howard, Duke of Norfolk and Lord Admiral, appointed William as his deputy to help defend the Norfolk and Suffolk coastline.

Then, in Henry VII's reign, William served on the commission of the peace in Kent, Norfolk, Westminster, Cambridge, East Dereham and Huntingdon. He also served as steward

Sir Wm Bullen K:B
1463

Sir Thomas Bullen K B
1506

and surveyor of West Thurrock in Essex and was appointed sheriff for Norfolk and Suffolk.[21] In 1492, William was part of a force that included his father-in-law, and that accompanied the king to France, where they laid siege to Boulogne. He was back in England in 1493, and in 1494 was at the royal court celebrating the young Prince Henry, the future Henry VIII, being made Duke of York.

By the end of 1486, William was even more important and wealthy, having inherited further lands from his mother and maternal grandfather. In 1497, William and his eldest son, Thomas, were part of the king's army that was victorious over the Cornish rebels at the Battle of Blackheath. Not long after this victory, Thomas Boleyn married Elizabeth Howard, the eldest daughter of Thomas Howard, Earl of Surrey, who would become 2nd Duke of Norfolk. The couple settled at the Boleyn estate in Blickling, Norfolk. It was at Blickling Hall that King Henry VII visited the Boleyns while on progress in 1498. Most intriguingly, the details in King Henry VII's Privy Purse Expenses tell us that the king visited a 'Mr Bolen', and not 'Sir' William, which, as Lauren Mackay argues, suggests that the king was visiting Thomas Boleyn. It was a great honour to host the monarch while he was on progress, and it would have cost the Boleyns dearly. What this visit signified was that the Boleyns were well and truly on the rise. Thomas Boleyn had secured a third advantageous marriage into the nobility for the Boleyns, and he was increasingly inching closer to the king.

21 Dean (1987), pp. 18, 26, 27; Calendar of the Fine Rolls, XXII, p. 295; Calendar of the Patent Rolls, Henry VII, II, pp. 645 and 651.

PREVIOUS PAGES: The arms of William Boleyn and Thomas Boleyn in Hever Castle's long gallery. Hever Castle's portrait of King Henry VII, 16th century.

In a later letter to Thomas Cromwell, Thomas Boleyn wrote of the financial hardship of the early years of his marriage, when Elizabeth brought him "every year a child" and they had just £50 to live on.[22] Thomas's fortunes improved in 1505 when his father, Sir William Boleyn, died, and Thomas inherited the manors of Blickling, Calthorpe, Wikmere, Mekylberton, Fylby, West Lexham, Possewick and Stiffkey, as well, of course, as Hever Castle. William was laid to rest in Norfolk Cathedral.

In truth, we have little evidence about Thomas and Elizabeth's day-to-day lives in these early years at Hever, although we can explore other kinds of evidence to reconstruct what their lives at the castle were probably like. It has even been disputed that Thomas used Hever much in the years before Anne Boleyn's rise, after which we can be far more certain that Thomas, Elizabeth, Anne, George, and George's wife Jane, were frequently in residence there. However, Thomas himself stated in 1538, in relation to a crime in Kent, that in the "...33 years" he had resided in Kent, he had known of no comparable act committed by his folk, suggesting that he had based himself in Kent from 1505.[23] Earlier correspondence in 1517 referred to Thomas as "Sir Th. Boleyn of Hever, Kent", and in 1523, he would again be referred to as "dwelling in Kent."[24] We have good evidence, too, that Thomas was a good steward to the Weald and took his stewardship of Penshurst seriously, overseeing the restoration of Tonbridge Castle and the reroofing of Penshurst Place.[25]

Hever was situated at the epicentre of the social worlds of the Boleyns, and the evidence points to Thomas and Elizabeth's family often frequenting the property. It was their closest property to London. Geoffrey Boleyn had created a family seat for the Boleyns at Blickling Manor. Thomas Boleyn made Hever the Boleyn family headquarters.

---

22 Letters and Papers, Foreign and Domestic, Henry VIII (L&P), Volume XI, 17, Earl of Wiltshire to Cromwell, July 1536.

23 L&P, XIII, 937, Earl of Wiltshire to Cromwell, 6 May 1538.

24 L&P, II, 3281; L&P, Addenda. Vol. 1: Part I, p.234.

25 L&P, IV, 1550., Thos. Lord Rocheford to Sir John Daunce, 8 August 1525.

The Boleyns and their Children
(1505-1521)

Sir Thomas Boleyn

On the Rise

WHILE BLICKLING remained the ancestral seat of the Boleyns, Hever emerged as the family home. By the time Thomas and Elizabeth settled with their young family in Kent, Thomas was well on the rise. The royal visit to Blickling had been an honour, albeit an expensive one, but it signified the beginnings of a career serving the Tudor kings.[26] Thomas may well have been with his father, William, who was chosen to be part of the entourage led by Henry, Duke of York, the future Henry VIII, to receive Katherine of Aragon on her arrival in England in 1501. We can be sure that Thomas was present when Katherine married Prince Arthur by proxy a couple of weeks later.

One of Hever Castle's current treasures is an easel painting of Prince Arthur commissioned by King Henry VII for Arthur's new bride, Katherine, as an engagement token. It remained in Katherine's possession and consequently was inherited by King Henry VIII. Arthur is depicted in princely, bejewelled attire and is holding a gillyflower (carnation), a token of betrothal. It is believed to be the only extant portrait of Arthur made in his lifetime, and it is an earlier example of a royal portrait than any held in the National Portrait Gallery.[27] Its presence at Hever Castle is particularly pertinent because Arthur died suddenly on 2nd April 1502. Henry VII's 'spare', Prince Henry, would take the throne in Arthur's place. Had Arthur survived, life would have been radically different for the Boleyn family. It is doubtful that the conditions in which the seismic events that facilitated the Boleyn's path to the throne would have existed had Arthur lived.

26 Mackay (2018), p. 25. Mackay points out that the records refer to "Mr Boleyn" rather than "Sir".
27 For a full analysis of this portrait of national importance, see Mould, P. 'Portrait of Prince Arthur of Wales, c.1500', [http://www.historicalportraits.com/Gallery.asp?Page=Item&ItemID=21&Desc=Arthur-Prince-of-Wales-%7C--English-School]

The arms of Thomas Boleyn, held in Hever's archive

Two years later, Thomas was part of Margaret Tudor's escort for her journey to Scotland to marry King James IV in 1503.[28] In the records for Henry VII's funeral in 1509, Thomas Boleyn is mentioned as an esquire of the body, and he continued serving the new seventeen-year-old king, Henry VIII, in that position.[29] Thomas and Elizabeth were honoured with privileged positions at Henry VIII's coronation celebrations in June 1509. Thomas was created a Knight of the Bath at the Tower of London's ancient bathing ceremony, and Elizabeth was appointed to serve the new queen, Katherine of Aragon, as one of the baronesses of the queen's chamber for her coronation.[30] Then, just over a month later, Thomas was appointed keeper of the Foreign Exchange in England and keeper of the Exchange in Calais.[31] He also served as sheriff for Norfolk and Suffolk for that year and the next, suggesting a considerable amount of movement for Thomas between his properties. With Elizabeth at court and Thomas between estates, it is possible that the Boleyn children were being educated at Hever.

Thomas was clearly a man the new king liked to have around him, for he was one of those who accompanied the king dressed as outlaws when Henry decided to surprise his queen and her ladies. The surprise was followed by dancing and entertainment.[32] The language of courtly love, speaking to notions of chivalry, was obviously a skill in which Thomas was fully conversant, and it was a skill that would be taught to his children. Thomas was also an active jouster and was one of those listed as taking part in the famous Westminster Tournament Challenge that celebrated the birth of Henry, Duke of Cornwall, son of King Henry VIII, in 1511. Sadly, the infant only lived for fifty-two days, and Thomas served as a chief mourner and knight bearer at the funeral.[33] This loss was a devastating blow for Queen Katherine, and it would be the first of many tragic losses for her.

---

28 Lelandi (1770), Volume IV, p. 265; *The manuscripts of His Grace the Duke of Rutland: preserved at Belvoir Castle* (1888), Volume I, p. 18; Dean (1987), p. 28.

29 L&P I, 20, Henry VII's funeral.

30 *Ibid.*, 81, Preparations for the Coronation; Ibid., 82, The Coronation.

31 *Ibid.*, 122, 132 (92).

32 Hall (1809), p. 513.

33 L&P I, 698.

The Boleyn Children

THOMAS AND Elizabeth Boleyn had five children. Mary was likely the eldest, born c.1499/1500, and Anne followed in c.1501. George, Thomas Boleyn's eventual heir, was born c. 1504. Thomas and Henry Boleyn's birth dates are far less clear, but they likely died in childhood, for they do not feature in the historical record. They are buried at Penshurst and Hever, respectively. The younger Thomas Boleyn's burial at Penshurst may suggest that he had been boarded out to the superior property to share a tutor, for Penshurst was then owned by the Duke of Buckingham, whose son Henry had been born in 1501, though this is conjecture. It would be next to Henry Boleyn, his lost son, that Thomas would be laid to rest many years later. Although Mary, Anne and George were probably born at Blickling, Hever is the property they would have called home, and they would have received their early education there.

The first room in the Boleyns' Solar - the family apartments on the first floor at Hever Castle - has a long tradition of being Anne Boleyn's bedroom. In Hever's archive are references to this space being traditionally the bedchamber of Anne dating back to the late seventeenth and early eighteenth centuries. It is possible that Anne Boleyn shared this small space with her sister Mary and perhaps a governess. It is also likely that as young children, the Boleyns all bedded down together on truckle beds in the great chamber, for this was a multifunctional space that could easily be adapted throughout the day with the shifting of furniture. It is likely that it was in this space that Elizabeth Boleyn oversaw the beginnings of her children's education, and we know from later correspondence from Anne to her father Thomas that he was also playing an active role in her education during these formative years. There were also rooms for the growing children in the castle's keep, which the offset gatehouse had made a comfortable size.

'Anne Boleyn's Bedroom' today

NEXT PAGE: Hever Castle's portraits of Anne Boleyn and Mary Boleyn, after Holbein, 18th century

It appears that Thomas Boleyn shared Thomas More's views that daughters should be educated in the same way as sons, proper 'learning', rather than simply focusing on virtue and domestic skills, so Anne, and her sister Mary, may well have been educated with their brother. George could speak Latin and Italian, and French, so Anne probably had some grounding in those languages. This was not a typical education for girls to receive, and it appears that Anne Boleyn flourished. Our only surviving piece of evidence from Mary, a letter, shows her to be assured and erudite. Thomas's own successes came from the skills he had learned and the opportunities afforded to him, and it very much appears that Thomas ensured that his children had the very best possible start in life.

Thomas's closeness to the king and the good service he had provided was recognised in the number of grants and offices he received in 1511 and 1512, including the keepership of a Nottinghamshire park and several manors in the counties of Essex, Hertfordshire, Surrey and Kent. With his neighbour, Henry Wyatt, he was granted the office of constable and keeper of the castle and gaol of Norwich. He was also granted one half of the custody of the lands, wardship and marriage of John, son and heir of Sir George Hastings. He was also reconfirmed and granted in survivorship, with his wife, Elizabeth, the manor of Wykmer in Norfolk. [34]

---

34 *Ibid.*, 709 (19); 833 (14) and (60); Morant (1763), Volume II, pp. 13, 92; Dean (1987), pp. 35-36; L&P I, 1083 (26), 1221 (27) and 1415 (4).

Prized Opportunities

THOMAS WAS an intelligent man with a gift for languages. This gift, combined with his skills in diplomacy and his position as a royal favourite, led to him being sent with John Young and Sir Robert Wingfield to the court of Margaret of Austria in 1512 and 1513 to conclude an alliance between England and Margaret's father, Maximilian I, the Holy Roman Emperor, against France.[35] Thomas made quite an impression on Margaret, and they became so friendly that they had a wager on how long the negotiations would take. Thomas's talent and speed at negotiating, which he managed in ten days, led to him winning the wager and earning himself Margaret's Spanish courser.[36] His good relationship with Margaret also led to him securing a place for his daughter, Anne, at her court. A place at Margaret's court was highly sought after by royal and noble families in Europe, so this showed just how much Margaret respected Thomas and how much Thomas valued his daughter's education.[37] It was a bold move from Thomas, and it gave Anne immense opportunity.

Anne left England for Margaret's court at Mechelen in the summer of 1513. Belgian historian, Ghislain de Boom, described Margaret's palace as "un école d'éducation princière et un centre de haute civilisation" ("a princely school and a centre of high culture/advanced civilisation"), so it was a wonderful opportunity for Anne, and she was appointed a tutor to help her improve her French.[38] Our first glimpse of Anne Boleyn's voice comes in the form of a letter that Anne sent to her father, possibly to Hever Castle. It shows Anne to be engaged in learning and full of gratitude for the opportunities that Thomas had secured for her. Concerned that her father would disapprove of errors in her French, she assures him that the letter is of her own

35 L&P I, Preface to the First Edition, p. LVIII; Dean (1987), pp. 36-38.

36 L&P I, 1338.

37 Paget (1981), pp. 162–170.

38 *Ibid.*, quoting Ghislaine de Boom, *Marguerite d'Autriche–Sauoie et la Pré–Renaissance* (Paris and Brussels).

autography and that she wished to perfect the skills 'enjoyed' upon her by Thomas.[39] The letter is a remarkable survival, for the few surviving letters written by Anne are from a later period, her time as the king's sweetheart and her queenship. Historian Lauren MacKay has suggested that the letter's survival may indicate that it was a treasured possession of Thomas. It certainly adds weight to the understanding that Anne and Thomas were close and that she was flourishing because of the opportunities he had achieved for her.

Back in England, 1514 saw more rewards for Thomas. By this time, Thomas owned, or had been granted, the controlling interest in around twenty manors, and he was the keeper of various other estates, as well as being keeper of the Exchange at Calais and the Foreign Exchange in all English ports. He was a wealthy and important man.[40]

In 1514, Thomas was also able to secure places for both of his daughters as maids of honour to eighteen-year-old Mary Tudor, King Henry VIII's sister, who was travelling to France to marry fifty-two-year-old King Louis XII. Thomas wrote to Margaret of Austria in August 1514 explaining the situation and asking her to release Anne and send her back to England with a chaperone. It seems likely that Mary Boleyn travelled with the princess to France, but Anne met them in France as she did not have enough time to get to England.[41] The French king died on 1st January 1515, and King Francis I inherited the throne. Mary Tudor married Charles Brandon, Duke of Suffolk, secretly in France before the couple headed back to England. It appears that Mary Boleyn travelled back to England with her royal mistress, but Anne was appointed to serve Francis I's wife, Queen Claude, as one of her maids of honour.

At the French court, Anne Boleyn's love of art, architecture and illuminated manuscripts grew. As Olivia Longueville's research has demonstrated, Anne grew up in a young and vibrant court, Queen Claude being but sixteen years of age when Anne entered her service. Anne was exposed to exquisite religious manuscripts, privy performances of music and court festivities. It

---

39 The letter is held at Corpus Christi College, (Cambridge, Corpus Christi College, MS 119: Letters Principally of Foreign Reformers).

40 Dean (1987), p. 48.

41 Ives, p. 27.

Hever Castle's copy of a letter from Thomas Boleyn to Margaret of Austria.
NEXT PAGE: Hever Castle's Wedding Tapestry, c.1525.

Original & very important holograph letter from Sir Thomas Boleyn [1477-1539] to Margaret of Austria asking her to allow his daughter "la petite boulain" to return to him as Mary Tudor desired to have her near her

1514

Aug 14.

Ma treschiere et tres redoubtee dame dans sy hūble cuer quil mest possible a vr̄e bonne grace me Recom̄ande. Il vous playra a sauoir com̄ent la seur du Roy mon maistre madame marie Reyne fyancee de france ma Requys de dauoir auecques elle ma fille la petitte boulain laquelle ma tresredoubtee dame ~~est a present auecques vous en vr̄e court a laquelle Requeste Je nay peu ne oceut~~ Refuzer nullement. si est ma tresredoubtee dame que Je vous supplie tres humblement quil vous plaise de doñer et octroyer congiet a ma fille de pouvoir Retourner pardevers moy auecques mes gens lesquels Jay envoyet devers vous a ceste cause ma tresredoubtee dame que Je ~~vous supplie~~ me tiens fort obligiet envers vr̄e bonne grace a cause de la grāt honeur que fait aues a ma fille, et que ne mest possible a desseruir devers vr̄e bonne grace non obstant que Je ne desire aultre chose synon que Je vo⁹ puisse faire aulcun seruice agreable ce que Jespere de faire encores cy en apres au plaisir de dieu auquel Je prie ma tres redoubtee dame quil vous doinst lentier accomplissement de vos nobles et bons desirs Escript desoubz mon signe manuel a la court Royalle de grynewichs en engleterre le xiiij Jour daoust lan xv^c et xiiij

Vr̄e tres hūble seruiteur

Sr Thoms Boleyn

A ma tres chiere et tresredoubtee Dame madame de savoye Regente et gouvernante de flandres &c

is also highly probable that Anne experienced the works of Leonard da Vinci, who had been employed to provide decorations for the dauphin's christening in 1516.[42] Anne was situated at the very heart of the Renaissance culture with which King Henry VIII strove to imbue his court. She adopted the freer and more flattering French fashions, although a commonplace myth suggests that Anne introduced the French Hood to the English court when we have sound evidence for its use beforehand. Similarly, it is maintained that Anne wore only the French fashions when we know she also wore the English ones. There was far more to Anne's 'Je ne sais quoi' than the cut of her hood. Anne was different because of the exposure she had gained to different ideas and new ways of thinking. She was fiercely intelligent, and even her opponents were captivated by what she had to say. To Henry, Anne had been moulded into the quintessence of the image he was determined to project for himself.

Thomas Boleyn had set about introducing his son George to the English court. The first mention of George at the royal court is at Christmas and New Year 1514/1515, when he and his father participated in a mummery, and he was appointed as a page shortly after.[43] George was entering court as his father had done, and he would benefit from the many skills of court etiquette and diplomacy in which Thomas excelled.

In 1516, Thomas attended the christening of Henry VIII's daughter, Mary, and acted as a canopy bearer.[44] Then, in 1517, he was entrusted with looking after the king's eldest sister, Queen Margaret of Scotland, the woman he'd escorted to Scotland fourteen years previously, on her visit to England. Margaret stayed for forty days, and during that time, Thomas acted as her official carver.[45] By 1518, Thomas was a member of the privy council and a respected ambassador, being involved in Cardinal Wolsey's negotiations for the Treaty of Universal Peace. Thomas was said to be the best French speaker at court, and this, plus his talent for diplomacy, led to him being appointed as the English ambassador to the French court. While he was in France, Thomas

42 See Olivia Longueville's 2020 article 'Anne Boleyn's Education and Life at the French Court'.

43 L&P II, pp. 1500-1502, Revels; Starkey (1974), pp. 139-140.

44 L&P II, 1573.

45 Ibid., p. 1475, The King's Book of Payments, 1517.

became close to the royal family. In 1519, he was taken to see the pregnant Queen Claude by the French king's mother, Louise of Savoy. Then at the subsequent christening of Henry, Duke of Orléans, Thomas sponsored the French king's infant son in the name of Henry VIII, presenting to Queen Claude a salt from the English king.[46]

46 L&P III, 289.

Miniatures of King Francis I, Marguerite of Angoulême and Queen Claude, 18th century.

Gold and Glory

THOMAS RETURNED to England in 1520 and was appointed comptroller of the household. But he was soon back in France to help plan and attend the historic Field of Cloth of Gold meeting between Henry VIII and Francis I in June 1520. Thomas was chosen as one of forty select members of government, nobility and church who rode with the king to his first meeting with his French counterpart. In addition, Thomas's wife, Elizabeth, and daughter, Mary, who was married to William Carey, a member of the king's privy chamber, were chosen to attend Queen Katherine. Both Thomas and Elizabeth took attendants to France, and it is likely that their son, George, was among them, and Anne would have been present serving Queen Claude.[47] It was a historic summit and a jubilant Boleyn reunion.

By May 1521, Thomas was treasurer of the household, and he was also appointed to the special commission of oyer and terminer that tried his neighbour, Edward Stafford, Duke of Buckingham. Following Buckingham's fall and execution, Thomas was granted manors in Kent that had belonged to the duke, including the manor and park of Penshurst, just a stone's throw from Hever.[48] He'd also recently been granted manors in Oxfordshire and Essex, so he now owned around two dozen manors. The systems of court power that Thomas was operating within could be brutal, and the blade had swung close to Hever when Buckingham had fallen. However, as Thomas's subsequent good fortune attested, power was generally gained from the downfalls of those once close to the king.

In 1521, Thomas accompanied Cardinal Wolsey to meet his old friend, Margaret of Austria, under the pretence of mediating between France and the Empire. The real purpose of the visit was to secure an alliance between England and the Empire, so this was a critical and sensitive diplomatic mission and showed just how much faith Wolsey and the king had in Thomas. With

---

47 Ibid., 702.

48 L&P III, ii, 2214 (29).

such a trusted position, it is important to stress that this stream of success on Thomas's part demonstrates that Thomas had already achieved status and wealth for his family through his own competence long before Anne Boleyn arrived at Henry VIII's court.

In 1520, negotiations began for a marriage between Thomas's daughter, Anne, and James Butler, son of Sir Piers Butler of Ireland. This marriage match would settle a dispute between Piers and Thomas, Thomas's mother and aunt, over the earldom of Ormond, a dispute that had started with the death of Thomas's maternal grandfather, Thomas Butler, 7th Earl of Ormond, in August 1515. The earl had no direct male heirs, but he left two daughters, Anne St Leger and Margaret Boleyn, and the Ormond title was entailed to heirs general, not just male heirs. However, while the earl had been at his estates in England, his Irish estates had been managed by his cousin, Sir James Butler, who came to regard the estates as his own. After his death and that of the earl, James's son, Piers, laid claim to the title and estate. He had the backing of the Irish lords and people, but Thomas Boleyn put forward his claim to the title and lands, and he had the backing of King Henry VIII. A solution needed to be found to keep the Boleyns and St. Legers happy, but also to keep the peace in Ireland, and Piers could help the English government control the troublesome Irish factions.

It is unclear who came up with the marriage idea, but correspondence between Thomas's brother-in-law, the Earl of Surrey, and the king suggests that it may have been Surrey's brainwave.[49] A marriage match between Anne Boleyn and James Butler would mean that the earldom of Ormond would pass to James and Anne on Piers's death and would therefore be in the Boleyn and Butler family. It would, however, mean that Thomas Boleyn would miss out, and it is hard to imagine Thomas being content with that. In late 1521, Anne was recalled from France to join Queen Katherine of Aragon's household and marry James.[50] Hever Castle was a far cry from the palaces that Anne Boleyn had become accustomed to, and she would go on to know the palaces of England far more intimately still. However, over the next ten years, Anne could often be found at Hever. Indeed, it often acted as her 'haven'.

---

49 LP III, 1004, 1011, 1762.

50 Calendar of State Papers, Spain: Further Supplement to Volumes 1 and 2, 30.

Haven
(1521-1533)

BY LATE 1521, Anne Boleyn, who had long been immersed in the cultures of the French court, had not seen her home of Hever Castle for nearly seven years. Indeed, the Boleyns were often to be found far from their Kentish family headquarters. The other Boleyn children had also taken flight from their childhood haven. George Boleyn took a permanent position at the royal court in around 1522, the year in which he received a joint grant with his father of offices that had belonged to their late neighbour, the Duke of Buckingham. Two years later, in 1524, George received his first grant in his own right, the Norfolk manor of Grimston, which may have been a wedding, or pre-wedding, present from the king, for George married Jane Parker, daughter of Henry Parker, Lord Morley, around this time.[51] The king himself made up part of Jane's dowry, and in return for the dowry of 2,000 marks, Thomas Boleyn guaranteed to give his daughter-in-law the rents of several manors, or an annual amount of 100 marks, should George predecease her.[52] Thus, Henry VIII was investing in the Boleyn family's good fortune, just as his father had.

Although George's marriage was an arranged one and was childless, we do not have any evidence that it was an unhappy one. Several authors and historians have successfully challenged the idea that Jane Boleyn helped bring down the Boleyn siblings in 1536 out of hatred and jealousy.[53]

George's new bride likely spent time with Elizabeth Boleyn at Hever Castle after their marriage. It was entirely customary for new brides to spend a period with their mother-in-law to get accustomed to managing their various manors. As George was the Boleyn heir, Hever Castle was destined to become George and Jane's property upon the death of Thomas and Elizabeth. This was a period of great mobility and prosperity for the Boleyns. The family were centred around the king and queen, making good marriages and reaping the benefits of

---

51 L&P IV, 546 (2).

52 L&P X, 1010; Fox (2007), pp. 36-38.

53 These include Julia Fox (Jane Boleyn, 2007), Charlie Fenton (Jane Parker: The Downfall of Two Tudor Queens?, 2021), Adrienne Dillard (The Raven's Widow: A Novel of Jane Boleyn, 2017), Clare Cherry and Claire Ridgway (George Boleyn: Tudor Poet, Courtier & Diplomat, 2014).

their achievements. In June 1525, in the same ceremony that the king's illegitimate son, Henry Fitzroy, was created Earl of Nottingham and Duke of Richmond and Somerset, Thomas Boleyn was created Viscount Rochford. Hever Castle had been the jewel of the portfolio of properties amassed by Thomas's grandfather. By the time Thomas assumed the title of viscount, he had amassed at least thirty manors and was still very much on the rise.

It was not all plain sailing for the Boleyns, however. George Boleyn lost his position in the privy chamber in Cardinal Wolsey's purge, the Eltham Ordinances, in 1526. The cardinal was concerned about the influence of the younger privy chamberers on the king, and removed them. George's compensation was an annual £20 payment and the position of cupbearer to the king.[54] Soon, George would rise once again, and his good fortunes, and bad, were irrevocably linked to those of his sister, Anne.

Anne Boleyn's first recorded appearance at Henry VIII's court was in March 1522, when she played Perseverance in the Shrovetide Château Vert pageant alongside her sister, Mary, as Kindness and her soon-to-be sister-in-law, Jane Parker, as Constancy.[55] It was a dazzling debut. Anne, in many ways, embodied the spirit of the Renaissance. Her education, begun at Hever with Thomas and Elizabeth, had developed in the Low Countries and latterly in France. She was equipped with eloquence of mind and manner that captivated many who encountered her. Although one of the reasons for her return was a potential marriage match with James Butler, Anne soon became involved with courtier Henry Percy, a member of Cardinal Wolsey's household and the son and heir of the Earl of Northumberland. According to George Cavendish, Wolsey's gentleman usher, Percy would "resort for his pastime unto the queen's chamber, and there would fall in dalliance among the queen's ladies, being at the last more conversant with Mistress Anne Boleyn than with any other" and soon "there grew such a secret love between them that, at length, they were ensured together, intending to marry."[56]

---

54 L&P IV, 1939 (12); Fox, p. 39.

55 Hall (1809), pp. 630-632.

56 Cavendish (1827), p. 121.

The king, however, found out about the romance and ordered Wolsey to put an end to it. Wolsey berated Percy for his "peevish folly" and called his father to court. The earl also gave the young man a dressing down.[57] The relationship was subsequently broken off, and Percy was forced to marry Mary Talbot, daughter of the Earl of Shrewsbury. Cavendish recorded that Anne was sent home to Hever Castle, "whereat she smoked" in frustration and nursed her broken heart.

Anne is next linked to poet and diplomat Thomas Wyatt the Elder, whose childhood home, Allington Castle, was not far from Hever. Wyatt had married Elizabeth Brooke in 1521, but it was an unhappy marriage. In his book on Anne Boleyn, Wyatt's grandson, George Wyatt, wrote of how his grandfather fell in love with Anne, and Wyatt's poetry supports this claim.[58] There's no evidence, however, that his feelings were returned, and his poem "Whoso list to hunt" suggests that Wyatt withdrew his pursuit of Anne when King Henry VIII came into the picture.

We do not know when Henry VIII became attracted to his wife's maid of honour, just that it was between 1524 and 1526. It coincided with the king's growing belief that his marriage to Katherine of Aragon was contrary to God's law, and that's why God was not blessing them with a surviving son. The king wrote Anne at least seventeen love letters between 1526 and 1528, and he used George Boleyn as a courier on at least one occasion, giving him further verbal messages to pass on to Anne.[59] It is clear from these letters that Henry was the aggressor. Anne left his first letters unanswered. She rebuffed him, even leaving court and retreating to Hever.

57 Ibid., p. 122.

58 His poem "What wourde is that that chaungeth not" has the answer "Anna", he writes of "That Brunet" in "The Lover Confesseth Him in Love with Phyllis" and in "Whoso list to hunt" he tells of a man hunting a hind (Anne), with little chance of success, and then being forced to withdraw from the hunt because of another hunter (Henry VIII).

59 Cherry & Ridgway (2014), p. 96.

Karen Lindsey has gone as far as to depict Anne Boleyn as a victim of sexual harassment, basing this idea on Wyatt's work:

> "Whoso list to hunt, I know where is an hind,
> But as for me, hélas, I may no more.
> The vain travail hath wearied me so sore,
> I am of them that farthest cometh behind.
> Yet may I by no means my wearied mind
> Draw from the deer, but as she fleeth afore
> Fainting I follow. I leave off therefore,
> Since in a net I seek to hold the wind.
> Who list her hunt, I put him out of doubt,
> As well as I may spend his time in vain.
> And graven with diamonds in letters plain
> There is written, her fair neck round about:
> Noli me tangere, for Caesar's I am,
> And wild for to hold, though I seem tame."

In this poem, which is based on Petrarch's "Una Candida Cerva", Wyatt starts with a challenge, telling those who want to hunt that he knows the location of a hind. Still, he goes on to say that he is weary of the chase and that his hunt failed, that Caesar claimed the hind: "Noli me tangere [don't touch me]," says the hind, "for I am Caesar's. This "wild to hold" hind can't be Wyatt's, she doesn't belong to him. It is thought that this poem is about Wyatt's feelings for Anne Boleyn, and, in an article in *The Guardian*, Carol Rumens writes:

"But this is still a love-poem, and nowhere more obviously than in that final, para-rhymed couplet, where, having quoted the injunction, Noli me tangere, the hind describes herself as "wild for to hold". This instantly transports us to a hinterland of erotic excitement, and registers the extent of the poet's loss and hurt, now that the King has claimed Wyatt's deer as his own."[60]

---

60 Rumens (2009).

It is a poem about lost love, but is Wyatt saying something even more by depicting Anne Boleyn as a hind? Is he seeing her as a quarry hunted down by the king, ensnared by him and becoming his whether she liked it or not? Being owned by him, even labelled by him as his possession? Perhaps that's reading too much into it, but Lindsey certainly sees Anne as Henry's victim, noting: "Today, Henry's approach to Anne would be instantly identifiable as sexual harassment. Anne, however, had no social or legal recourse against the man who ruled the country. She continued, as so many women before and since have done, to dodge her pursuer's advances while sparing his feelings. It didn't work… It was a hellish position […] To offer him the outright insult he asked for would be to risk not only her own but her father's and brother's careers at court." She points out that like the hind in Wyatt's poem, "Anne was a creature being hunted, and hunted by the king — like the buck he had killed and so proudly sent to her. There could be no refuge from the royal assault; no one would risk protecting her from Henry's chase. She could run, hide, dodge for a time, but the royal hunter would eventually track down his prey. And he would destroy her. The hunt was not an archaic metaphor in sixteenth century life, it was a vivid integral part of that life and everyone knew what happened to the wild creature at the end."[61]

Like any young Tudor woman, Anne knew the importance of keeping her virginity to make a good marriage match, and she was unwilling to be a king's mistress, even an official and recognised mistress, his *maîtresse-en-titre*. It is clear from the king's responses to Anne that she was offended by his suggestions, and he had to work hard to win her over. As Eric Ives has pointed out, Anne's refusal should have been the point at which the relationship "withered", when Henry could so easily have moved on to an easier conquest. Still, Henry's letters show "the king's realisation that he could not live without Anne, and therefore she, rather than some foreign princess, would have to be the wife to replace Katherine."[62]

Henry would not take no for an answer, and during the Christmas of 1526, Anne Boleyn and her family were back at Hever Castle for the festivities. Anne had either fallen for the king's

61 Lindsey (1996).

62 Ives (2004), p. 86.

MARCI
OMNI CREATVRE

charms or been worn down by his constant pursuit.[63] Perhaps Anne's presence at Hever could be explained by a desire on her part to ensure that an absence from the king would make his heart grow fonder. Perhaps she needed some respite from the endless gossip and discomfort at court. Lost to history are the many unequalled conversations had at Hever that Christmastide, for King Henry VIII had offered the unthinkable to Anne: his hand in marriage and the crown. At some point during that Christmas at Hever Castle, Anne made her decision. It is difficult to imagine a more consequential one.

Anne sent Henry a love token to symbolise her submission. The king wrote to her, saying "I thank you most cordially, not only on account of the fine diamond and the ship in which the solitary damsel is tossed about, but chiefly for the fine interpretation and the too humble submission which your goodness hath used towards me in this case." As Eric Ives has noted, "For centuries the ship had been a symbol of protection - the ark which rescued Noah from the destroying deluge; the diamond - as the Roman de la Rose had said - spoke of a 'heart as hard as diamond, steadfast and nothing pliant'. Anne was saying 'yes'." The gold and diamonds told Henry that Anne was prepared to brave the stormy waters ahead and voyage into the unknown, into the impossible. Everything changed for the Boleyns of Hever when Anne said 'yes' to the king. A few months later, the king applied for a dispensation to marry her.

A dispensation was necessary to cover the impediment of affinity, for at some point after she had returned with Mary Tudor from France in 1515, Mary Boleyn had become King Henry VIII's mistress. Although some historians date their affair to 1522, when Henry VIII rode out at the Shrovetide joust with the motto *"Elle mon Coeur a navera"*, or "She has wounded my Heart", embroidered on his horse's trappings, there is no evidence to link this to Mary. If their relationship worked like his affair with Elizabeth Blount, he slept with Mary and then arranged a good marriage match for her. Mary married William Carey, a member of the king's privy

63 David Starkey believes that Anne said "yes" to Henry VIII on 1st January 1527 by giving him a special New Year's gift, "the costly Diamond, and the Ship in which the solitary Damsel is tossed about". 'Henry VIII: The First Brexiteer', talk by Dr David Starkey at the Festival Theatre, Hever Castle, 8 August 2018; Ives (2004), pp. 88-90.

Hever Castle's portrait of King Henry VIII, after Joos van Cleve, c.1535

chamber, an esquire of the body, and a man related to the king, in February 1520, in a ceremony attended by the king.[64] The couple had two children, Catherine, born c.1524, and Henry, born in 1526.

By 1527, the year that Anne accepted the king's marriage proposal, Thomas Boleyn had become one of the wealthiest men in England. In an assessment of the subsidy on lands, the average peer was found to be worth £300-600, while Thomas was worth £800.[65] This was a huge amount and showed his importance and the esteem in which the king held him. He had carried out many important duties and successful embassies, and from 1527 he would be busy travelling on more diplomatic missions. However, these embassies would be closer to home in their mission; they were connected with the Great Matter, the king's quest for an annulment so that he could marry Thomas's daughter. Thomas carried these out to the best of his ability, but it does appear that he was initially against the idea of Anne marrying the king.[66]

Thomas and Elizabeth welcomed Anne back home at Hever for Christmas and New Year 1527/8. Anne may have been the king's fiancée, but Katherine of Aragon was still his official queen and, with her husband, presided over the entertainments of the Twelve Days of Christmas as such. Anne was still at Hever in February 1528, when she acted as host to diplomats Stephen Gardiner and Edward Fox, who were making their way to see the pope. In a letter to Anne, the king explained that the two men were "dispatched with as many things to compasse our matter, and to bring it to passe, as our wits could imagine or devise", commenting that he hoped he and Anne would shortly have their "desired end".[67] Anne had returned to court by the ambassadors' return in May, and she and the king were happy with their progress.

---

64 L&P III, p. 1539, The King's Book of Payments, 1520.

65 L&P IV ii, 2972.

66 Chapuys reported in February 1533 "I must add that the said earl of Wiltshire has never declared himself up to this moment; on the contrary, he has hitherto, as the duke of Norfolk has frequently told me, tried to dissuade the King rather than otherwise from the marriage." Calendar of State Papers, Spain, Volume 4 Part 2, 1531-1533, 1048.

67 The Harleian miscellany (1744), Volume III, p. 59.

On 16th June 1528, Anne was still at court when one of her maids caught sweating sickness, an illness that could kill in hours. Panic ensued. The royal court broke up, and Henry VIII and Katherine of Aragon fled London to Waltham Abbey, with George accompanying them as cupbearer. Meanwhile, Anne tried to escape the illness by making her way home to Hever. Unfortunately, George was taken ill at Waltham, and Anne and Thomas, who had already been at Hever, came down with the sweat. A panicked Henry VIII wrote to his fiancée, assuring her that he would send one of his physicians, Dr William Butts, to treat her:

"There came to me in the night the most afflicting news possible. For I have reason to grieve upon three accounts. First, because I heard of the sickness of my mistress, whom I esteem more than all the world, whose health I desire as much as my own, and the half of whose sickness I would willingly bear to have her cured. Secondly, Because I fear I shall suffer yet longer that tedious absence, which has hitherto given me all possible uneasiness, and, as far as I can judge, is like to give me more. I pray God he would deliver me from so troublesome a tormentor. The third reason is, because the physician, in whom I trust most, is absent at present, when he could do me the greatest pleasure. For I should hope by him, and his means, to obtain one of my principal joys in this world, that is, my mistress cured; however, in default of him, I send you the second, and the only one left, praying God that he may soon make you well, and then I shall love him more than ever. I beseech you to be governed by his advices with relation to your illness; by your doing which I hope shortly to see you again, which will be to me a greater cordial than all the precious stones in the world.

Written by the secretary who is, and always will be,
Your loyal and most assured Servant,
H. (A B) R."[68]

The outbreak was severe. At the end of June 1528, Jean du Bellay recorded that 2,000 people had died in London and wrote of how he had "sweated" at the Archbishop of Canterbury's house in Lambeth, and, while he was ill there, eighteen members of the archbishop's household had died in only four hours. Fortunately, George, Anne and Thomas Boleyn recovered from the

68 *Ibid.*, p. 57.

ān. Adoramus te christe ⁊ benedicimus ti
bi: quia per sanctam crucem tuaz redemi
sti mundum.

Domine iesu xp̄e fili dei viui pone Oremus.
passionē crucem ⁊ mortē tuaz inter
iudicium tuū ⁊ animas nostras nūc ⁊ in
hora mortis nostre: ⁊ largiri digneris vi
uis misericordiā ⁊ gratiā defūctis requiē
⁊ veniā / ecclesie tue pacem ⁊ concordiā ⁊
nobis peccatoribꝰ vitā ⁊ gloriā sempiter
nam. Qui viuis ⁊ regnas deus. Per oia
secula seculoꝝ. Amen.

Gloriosa passio dn̄i nostri iesu xp̄i eruat
nos a dolore tristi: ⁊ pducat nos ad gau
dia paradisi. Amen.

Ad septam de cōpassione vgi. Hyꝰ.

Ora sexta respicit mater suuz na
tum. Obsitum vulneribus in cru
ce leuatū. Inter fures positū felleqz pota
tum. Illa secum centies reddit eiꝰ latum.

ān. Te laudamus ⁊ rogamꝰ mater iesu
xp̄i. Ut intendas ⁊ defendas nos a mor
te tristi.

Domine sancte iesu fili dulcis vir Oremus.
ginis marie: qui p nobis mortē in
cruce tollerasti / fac nobiscū miam tuam:
⁊ da nobis ⁊ cunctis cōpassionez tue san
ctissime matris deuote recolētibꝰ eiꝰ amo
re vitā in presenti gratiosaz / ⁊ tua pieta
te gloriā in futuro sempiternam. Qui
viuis ⁊ regnas deꝰ. Per oia.

Ad nonam de beata maria.

Remeber me when you do pray
that hope doth led from day to day

Anne Boleyn

Deus in adiutorium meū in
tende. Dn̄e ad adiuuandū
me festina. Gloria patri ⁊
filio. Sicut erat. Hymnus.

Veni creator spiritus mentes tuoꝝ
Visita imple superna gratia que tu
creasti pectora. Memento salutis auctor
q̄ nostri quondā corporis ex illibata vir
gine nascendo formaz sumpseris. Maria
plena gratie mater misericordie tu nos ab

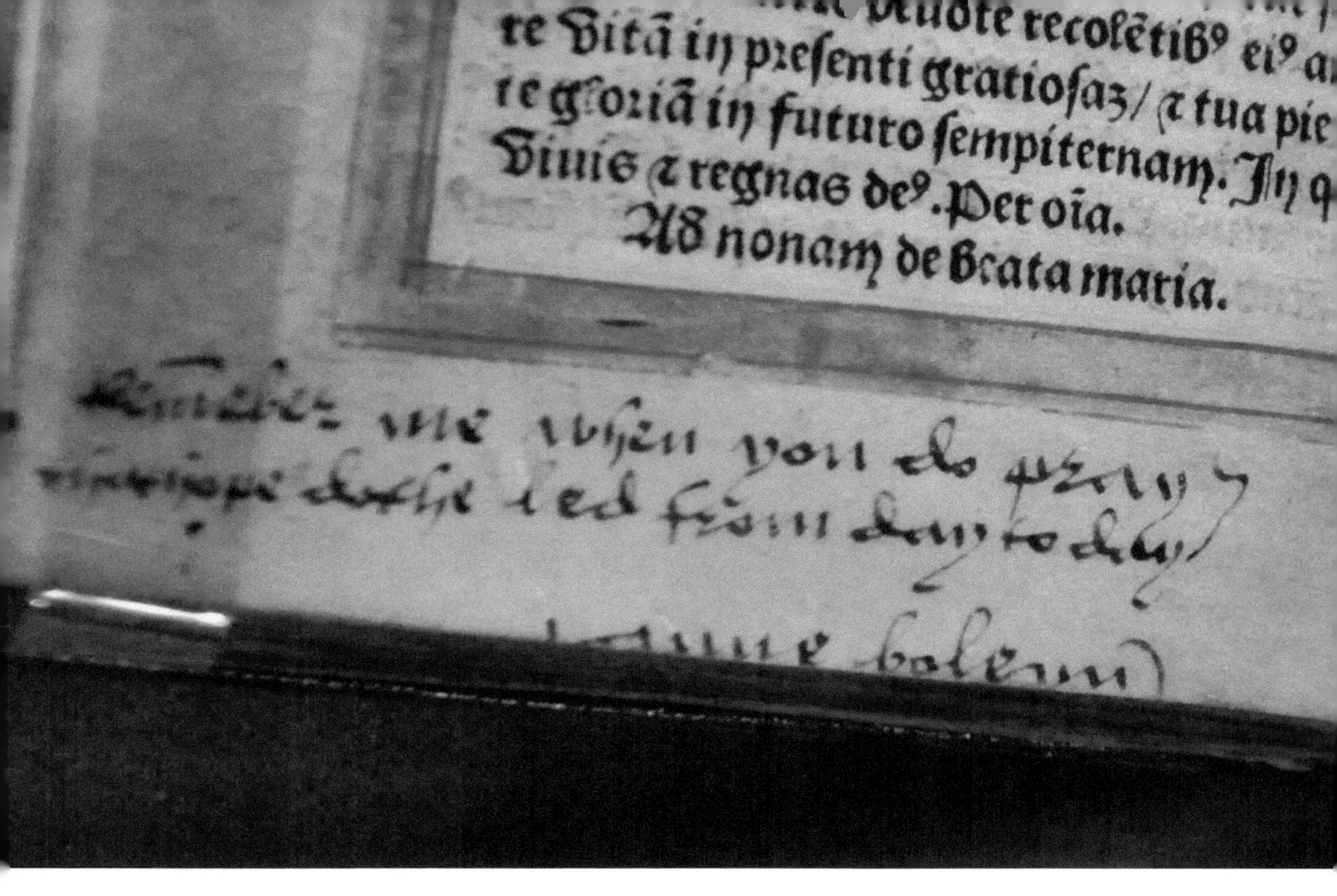

illness, but Mary Boleyn's husband, William Carey, died.[69] Mary was left in near poverty after her husband's death due to Carey's grants and offices reverting to the Crown. It appears that there had been a family breakdown between Mary and her parents, for the king himself had to intercede on Mary's behalf to obtain her father's help. Anne was able to help her sister, and Mary's two-year-old son, Henry, was made Anne's ward. Anne secured the service of French

69 L&P IV, 4440 and 4542; Hall (1809) p. 592.

Anne Boleyn's Book of Hours, c.1528 (Detail above)

scholar and reformer Nicholas Bourbon to tutor the young boy, and in December 1528, the king assigned Mary an annuity of £100 (£32,000), which had once been paid to her husband.

Mary might have been in the Boleyns' bad books, but George was busy making them proud. After he had recovered from sweating sickness, George continued in his service to the king. He was appointed Master of the Buckhounds and an esquire of the body. In late 1528, George was made keeper of the Palace of Beaulieu, and just two months later, chief steward of the palace.[70]

Following her illness, Anne planned initially to return to court with her mother towards the end of July. However, there is no mention of her father planning to accompany them, so perhaps he was still recovering. In the end, Thomas moved to Penshurst before returning to court, and Anne didn't return to London until the end of August. It was to be a short-lived return for Anne was sent back to Hever in September 1528 due to the imminent arrival of the papal legate, Cardinal Lorenzo Campeggio, who was being sent to England to hear the king's case for an annulment of his marriage. The king wanted Campeggio and the pope to believe that his conscience was troubled regarding his marriage, and he didn't want it to look as if he only wanted out of it so that he could marry Anne. His sweetheart was sent home, and he played man and wife with Katherine. Unfortunately, things didn't go to plan with Campeggio's visit. A special legatine court opened at Blackfriars in May 1529, presided over by Campeggio as legate and Cardinal Thomas Wolsey as the pope's vicegerent. However, it adjourned without making any ruling in July 1529, never to sit again. It was a huge blow for the king and the Boleyns.

Again and again, Hever played the role of Anne Boleyn's place of haven. As the Boleyns' impressive portfolio of manor houses grew, Hever retained a special place in the family's affections. It was compact enough to house Elizabeth and the children in their formative years, just large enough for the family. Now, the modest proportions of Hever proved to be beneficial in that they provided sanctuary and secrecy. Anne could place herself at Hever for weeks or months, and the limited capacity for visitors meant that she could close ranks during one of the

70 L&P IV, 4993 (15), 5248.

most turbulent periods of her life. Hever became not only her private sanctuary and her place of quarantine, but it acted as Anne's safety valve.

1529 was a good year in many respects for the Boleyns, though. The failure of the legatine court led to Wolsey being vulnerable to his enemies, men like the Dukes of Norfolk and Suffolk, Sir Thomas More, and the Boleyns, who were now convinced that Wolsey was not working for the annulment and was simply stalling. Wolsey fell from power and was replaced by Sir Thomas More. George Boleyn benefited from the cardinal's fall when he was granted annuities from his estates.

In late 1529, Anne's mother, Elizabeth, was at court with her daughter, playing chaperone. Chapuys records that Elizabeth accompanied Anne and the king to view York Place in October 1529, after Cardinal Wolsey had fallen from favour and the king had taken the palace: "The downfall of the Cardinal is complete. He is dismissed from the Council, deprived of the Chancellorship, and constrained to make an inventory of his goods in his own hand, that nothing may be forgotten. It is said that he has acknowledged his faults, and presented all his effects to the King. Yesterday the King returned to Greenwich by water secretly, in order to see them, and found them much greater than he expected. He took with him "sa mye" (his darling—Anne Boleyn), her mother, and a gentleman of his chamber (Norris?)." Elizabeth and Anne then made York Place their base, lodging in the chamber under the cardinal's former library.[71]

1529 saw the opening of the Reformation Parliament, the beginning of the break with Rome, and further rewards for the Boleyns. George was restored to the king's privy chamber, this time as a gentleman. He was also knighted and appointed governor of St Bethlehem Hospital.[72] In December 1529, Thomas Boleyn was granted the earldoms of Wiltshire and Ormond while George became Lord Rochford. Then, in January 1530, Thomas was made keeper of the privy seal, and the Boleyn men were sent on embassy - Thomas to Bologna to plead the king's case for an annulment to the pope and Emperor Charles V, and George to Paris to collect the opinions of

---

71 *Ibid.*, 6026; Ives (2004) p. 146.
72 L&P IV, 5815 (27).

HONY SOYT
Sir Thomas Bullen
Erle of Wilscher and Ormunde 1529

learned theologians on the king's situation.[73] Thomas's mission was a failure, but martyrologist John Foxe tells an amusing story about this mission. According to Foxe, the pope, who was seated under his cloth of estate, stuck out his foot for Thomas and the other diplomats to kiss, when Thomas's dog, a "great spaniel", "took fast with his mouth the great toe of the pope", much to the amusement of the Englishmen present.[74] The failure of his mission, and the treatment he received from the pope and emperor, made Thomas support the idea of a break with Rome all the more.

In June 1530, a deposition signed by the Lords Spiritual and Temporal, which included George Boleyn, was sent to the pope, praying him to consent to the king's request for an annulment and pointing out the evils that could arise from a delay in granting this request. Henry VIII was still convinced that the pope would eventually grant him his request and that he simply needed to be made aware that the people of England supported it, but the king was wrong.

In the meantime, Anne Boleyn had been reading Bible translator William Tyndale's book *The Obedience of a Christian Man*. It was deemed a heretical work and ended up being confiscated from the sweetheart of one of Anne's ladies by Dr Sampson, Dean of the Chapel Royal, after Cardinal Wolsey had commanded him to keep an eye out for such works of heresy. On hearing of the confiscation from her panicked lady, Anne went to the king to ask him to intervene with Wolsey to get the book returned. When the book was returned to her, Anne took it to the king and "besought his Grace most tenderly to read it." George Wyatt writes of how she had marked matters "worthy of the King's knowledge" with her fingernail, and John Strype describes how the king was "delighted" with the book. He remarked that "This Book is for me and all Kings to read." Strype goes on to say:

"And in a little Time the King by the Help of this virtuous Lady, by the Means aforefaid, had his Eyes opened to the Truth, to search the Truth, to advance God's Religion and Glory, to abhor the Pope's Doctrine, his Lies, his Pomp and Pride, to deliver his Subjects out of the

73 *Ibid.*, 6163 (1).

74 Fox, John (1851), pp. 632-633.

The Arms of Thomas Boleyn as Earl of Wiltshire and Ormond in Hever's long gallery.

henry [illegible]

George Rocheford

Wyllyam Weston

[illegible]

Egyptian Darkness, the Babylonian Bonds, that the Pope had brought him and his Subjects under. And so contemning the Threats of all the World, the Power of Princes, Rebellions of his Subjects at Home, and the raging of so many and mighty Potentates abroad; set forward a Reformation in Religion, beginning with the Triple Crowned Head at first, and so came down to the Members, Bishops, Abbots, Priors, and such like."[75]

Although Tyndale ended up being executed as a heretic during Henry VIII's reign, his book was instrumental in helping the king see how he could have his marriage to Katherine of Aragon annulled while also limiting the power of the papacy in England. With the pope not playing ball, Henry and his advisors turned to Parliament and Convocation.

In February 1531, Convocation granted the king the title of "singular protector, supreme lord, and even, so far as the law of Christ allows, supreme head of the English church and clergy", and it was George Boleyn, who played a prominent role in persuading Convocation of the scriptural case for the king's supremacy. He'd been sent to Convocation to express the king's growing anti-papal sentiments and Parliament's arguments for the supremacy, taking several tracts with him. Although Convocation initially baulked at the idea of proclaiming the king head of the church, they were happy when the title was tempered with the words "as far as the law of Christ allows". This was a big step towards the break with the authority of Rome. A year later, George participated in a meeting with the clergy to demand their submission, and another one to receive their formal submission.

---

75 Wyatt, G., *The Life of Anne Boleigne*. This appears in Cavendish (1825), Volume II; Strype (1822) Volume I, Part I, pp. 172-173.

The signature of George Boleyn, Viscount Rochford.
NEXT PAGE: Hever Castle's Marriage Plaque.

Howard

Hen·VIII ⁊ Boleyn

Things were looking good for the king and Anne now, and a visit was planned for the couple to travel to Calais to meet with King Francis I of France to gain his support for their marriage. But first, Henry VIII wanted to ensure that his fiancée was of sufficient standing for him to introduce to the French king as his betrothed. On 1st September 1532, in a ceremony attended by her father at Windsor Castle, Anne was elevated to the peerage. She was created Marquess of Pembroke in her own right and granted lands with an income of over £1,000.[76] Renovation work began on the royal lodgings of the Tower of London, lodgings that tended to be used before a royal coronation, and Katherine of Aragon was stripped of the royal jewels so that they could be given to Anne to wear on the trip to Calais. The royal couple set sail from Dover bound for Calais on 11th October, accompanied by an entourage which included Thomas Boleyn and his brothers, Sir James and Sir Edward; George and his wife, Jane, and Mary Boleyn, Lady Carey. Following meetings between the two kings in Boulogne, the two sovereigns arrived back at Calais on 25th October, Francis armed with a diamond as a gift for Anne. Anne played host to the French king at a lavish masquerade and banquet on the 27th, a celebration of the kings' good relationship and Francis's approval for Henry and Anne's marriage plans.[77] The trip couldn't have been more successful and, according to chronicler Edward Hall, on their return to England, on 14th November 1532, the Feast of St Erkenwald, Henry and Anne were married.[78]

---

76 L&P V, 1274: 3, 6.; Hall (1809), p. 790.

77 Hall (1809), pp.792-793; Wynkyn de Worde, (1885), pp.14-15.

78 Hall (1809), p. 794.

OVER: Hever Castle's Marriage Plaque.

The Thousand Days
(1533-1540)

ANNA BOLINA · ANG · REGINA

HENRY AND Anne were not in any hurry to journey back to London following their secret marriage, with the king deciding to spend a few days in Dover and the surrounding area "for the purpose of having harbours constructed in the said town, or at least of creating a specious plea for asking money from his subjects for the said works". They eventually arrived at Eltham Palace on 24th November,[79] and it was from that point that the couple began co-habiting.

On the Feast of the Conversion of St Paul, 25th January 1533, the couple underwent another secret marriage. Soon to be Bishop of Coventry and Lichfield, Rowland Lee, officiated at the ceremony at Whitehall, formerly York Place, the property the couple had refurbished following the fall of its previous owner, Cardinal Wolsey. Nicholas Harpsfield, the Catholic apologist, writing in Mary I's reign, recorded that the king and queen were attended by Henry Norris and Thomas Heneage, of the king's privy chamber, and Anne Savage, Lady Berkeley. Eustace Chapuys, reporting on the marriage a month later, recorded wrongly that Thomas Cranmer had officiated and went on to say that the royal couple married "in the presence only of her father, mother, brother, and two intimate female friends of the Lady herself, besides a priest of the diocese of Canterbury".[80]

According to Harpsfield, although the king's marriage to Katherine of Aragon had not yet been annulled, Henry assured Rowland Lee that "he had gotten of the Pope a lycence to marry another wife". When Lee asked to see the licence on the day of the marriage, the king said he had one, "but it is reposed in another sure[r] place whereto no man resorteth but myself, which, if it were seen, should discharge us all." Lee either had to take the king at his word or risk upsetting him by asking to see the licence. Lee chose to go ahead with the ceremony.

Anne may not have been aware at the time of her marriage that she was pregnant, but she soon guessed. Paul Friedmann, citing Chapuys, gives an account of Anne's behaviour at court on 22nd February 1533: "[...] she came out of her apartment into the hall where a large company was assembled. Seeing one of her favourite courtiers (Thomas Wyatt, probably), she abruptly

---

79 Calendar of State Papers, Spain, IV ii. 1030.

80 Harpsfield (1878), pp. 234-235.

told him that three days ago she had felt such a violent desire to eat apples as she had never felt before, that when she had spoken of it to the king he had said it was a sign that she was with child, but that she had replied it was not. Thereupon she broke into a violent fit of laughter."[81]

Friedmann comments that those who heard her concluded that Anne was either married or would be married soon, for they obviously had not yet heard of her wedding. Anne had also been reported as telling her uncle, the Duke of Norfolk, "in open court" that she would go on a pilgrimage straight after Easter if she weren't pregnant soon.[82] Anne wasn't concerned about who heard that she was pregnant or trying to be so.

Even though Anne was married to the king, Henry had not yet obtained an annulment of his first marriage, so this needed to be rectified as soon as possible. On 15th March 1533, Chapuys reported to the Emperor that "the King has had a chaplain, and the Lady also one of hers, to preach before them that all the time he had lived with his Queen he had been in adultery and sin, and that all his good subjects ought to pray God to forgive him such an offence, and enlighten him so as to take soon another wife" and that this wife could be "of low rank, provided the virtues and secret merits of the person thus chosen should counterbalance her position, as happened in the cases of kings Saul and David." Of course, Henry had already married Anne.

On 14th March, a Bill in Restraint of Appeals was introduced in the Commons. This bill prohibited appeals to Rome on legal or other matters, and it was this act that began the process of the transfer of authority from Rome to the king when it was subsequently passed. On 30th March 1533, Thomas Cranmer, a man patronised by the Boleyns, was consecrated as Archbishop of Canterbury. His first duty was to preside over the Convocation meeting to discuss the validity of Henry VIII's marriage to Katherine, his brother's widow. On 5th April 1533, Convocation gave its ruling, stating that the pope had no power to dispense in the case of a man marrying his brother's widow and that it was contrary to God's law. Katherine of Aragon was informed on 9th April that she had been demoted from queen consort to Dowager Princess of Wales, a title that she never recognised.

---

81 Friedmann, (1884), p. 190.

82 *Ibid.*, p. 189.

Hever Castle's silver replica of the Marriage Clock gifted by Henry VIII to Anne Boleyn.

At the end of March, Anne Boleyn's royal household was formed, and on 11th April 1533, Good Friday, King Henry VIII informed his royal council that Anne Boleyn was now his wife and that they must accord her with royal honours. On Easter Eve, Anne Boleyn attended mass in the Queen's Closet at Greenwich Palace "with all the pomp of a Queen, clad in cloth of gold, and loaded (carga) with the richest jewels" and attended by sixty ladies.[83]

Convocation's ruling on the dispensation was followed by a trial at a special court that opened on 10th May 1533 at Dunstable Priory, Bedfordshire, to examine Henry VIII's case for the annulment of his first marriage. It was presided over by Cranmer, who announced the sentence on 23rd May 1533, declaring the marriage to be "against the law of God" and annulling the marriage. On 28th May 1533, Cranmer proclaimed the validity of Henry VIII's marriage to Anne Boleyn after a special inquiry at Lambeth Palace. It was just in time for Anne's coronation.

The Tower of London had been specially refurbished for Anne's sojourn before her coronation procession. On 29th May 1533, four days of celebrations for Queen Anne Boleyn's coronation began in earnest with a river pageant on the Thames and ending with a coronation ceremony and banquet on 1st June. The six-month-pregnant Anne Boleyn was crowned queen at Westminster Abbey by Archbishop Cranmer. Her brother and uncle were busy on an embassy in France, but her father escorted her to and from the ceremony. Thomas must have watched in amazement as St Edward's crown, which was normally reserved for the crowning of a monarch, was placed on his daughter's head. It was a triumphant moment for the Boleyns.

On 26th August 1533, at Greenwich Palace, Anne took to her chamber to prepare for the birth of her baby. A healthy daughter, the future Queen Elizabeth I, was born on 7th September. George missed the christening on 10th September, having returned to France to prevent a meeting between the French king and the pope, but Thomas, the undoubtedly proud grandfather, helped hold the infant princess's train.

---

83 Calendar of State Papers Relating To English Affairs in the Archives of Venice, Volume 4, 1527-1533, 870.

The arms of Queen Anne Boleyn in Hever Castle's long gallery.

Queen Anne Boleyn 1533

A year which had seen Anne's marriage to the king, her coronation and the birth of a healthy baby must have been such a blessing to the Boleyns after all those years of frustration, disappointment and waiting. In 1533 and 1534, the Boleyns were at their zenith of power. Thomas was rewarded with further grants, making him the owner of well over 40 manors. George was an established diplomat, carrying out important duties for the king and receiving grants and favours as rewards, such as being made Lord Warden of the Cinque Ports and Constable of Dover Castle.[84]

In March 1534, Parliament passed the First Act of Succession, declaring Anne's marriage to the king valid and establishing the line of succession through the line of Henry and Anne's children. The icing on the cake was that Anne was pregnant again. In July 1534, George was sent to France to reschedule a meeting between the royal couple and the French king due to his sister's pregnancy, but sadly Anne lost her baby. It must have been a bitter blow for Anne when her sister, Mary, turned up at court in that September visibly pregnant to inform the queen that she had married in secret. The Boleyns were furious with Mary's deceit. She was banished from court and had to resort to writing to Thomas Cromwell in the hope that he'd intercede with her family.[85]

In 1535, Thomas Boleyn was involved in the prosecutions of those who opposed the royal supremacy. He served on the commission that tried John Fisher, Bishop of Rochester, was one of those chosen to examine Sir Thomas More, and he and George were on the commission that tried More. They were also present at More's execution and those of the Carthusian monks of London Charterhouse. However, it was also in 1535 that Thomas appears to have decided to spend less time at court and more time at Hever, while George carried out his sixth and final diplomatic mission to France to negotiate a marriage match between his niece, Princess Elizabeth, and Francis I's third son. The mission was a failure.

1536 started well for the Boleyns. Anne was pregnant once more, and Thomas and George were delighted by news of the death of Katherine of Aragon on 7th January. However, on 26th

84 L&P VII, 922 (16).
85 ed. Wood (1846), pp. 193-197.

January, the king suffered a jousting accident. It was said that the shock of this, combined with news of the king's flirtation with Jane Seymour, led to Anne suffering a miscarriage on 29th January, losing a son. The miscarriage made Anne vulnerable to her enemies, the Catholic conservatives who supported the Lady Mary, Henry's daughter by Katherine of Aragon. Anne's disagreement with Thomas Cromwell over where the money from the dissolution of the monasteries went and her opposition to an alliance with the empire added to this vulnerability. Her husband was also heavily involved with Jane Seymour. According to the Imperial ambassador, Jane was being coached on how to appeal to the king and to tell him how unpopular his marriage to Anne was with the people.[86]

On 2nd May 1536, Anne was arrested at Greenwich Palace, and George was arrested at Whitehall. Anne had been watching a game of tennis when she was summoned before the council and detained in her apartments to await the turning tide. The journey by barge was an eerily familiar one. Barely a thousand days earlier, Anne had been rowed to the Tower of London in triumph for her coronation.[87] Did she remember Henry greeting her as she landed again at the same steps and as she entered the fortress through the Court Gate, now the Byward Postern, where he had once publicly embraced her?[88] It was not the king, but his Lieutenant of the Tower, Sir Edmund Walsingham, who greeted Anne now. We will never know if Anne was aware that

86 L&P X. 282; Calendar of State Papers, Spain, V: ii. 43.

87 See Ives (2004), p.334.

88 For many years the Yeoman Warders of the Tower have guided visitors to the infamous Traitors' Gate for the location where Anne was bought into the Tower. It is almost certain, however, that she landed at the Queen's steps and entered the Tower, as she had before her coronation, at the Court Gate, or Byward Postern.

An Irish 'harp' groat with the initials of Henry and Anne

she had just made her final journey, but we know that Anne had entreated her chaplain, Matthew Parker, to a certain duty of care for Elizabeth on 26th April, six days earlier.[89] Perhaps Anne had read the temperature at court and was aware that the winds were turning against her.

When she encountered Sir William Kingston, the Constable of the Tower, before the royal apartments, Anne asked: "Mr Kingston, shall I go into a dungeon?", to which Kingston replied: "No, Madam. You shall go into the lodging you lay in at your coronation." Anne knelt, weeping with the words "it is too g[ood] for me, Jesu have mercy on me", before falling "into a great laughing".[90] Anne was unravelling, and her actions over the next few days would prove fatal.

On her arrival at the Tower, Anne spoke of her concern for her mother, who'd recently been at court and who was recorded as being "sore diseased with the cough, which grieves her sore."[91] Amongst periods of melancholy and despair, Anne also displayed bouts of optimism during her imprisonment. Foremost in her mind, however, had been the question of what she had been accused and why. By allowing Anne to talk and consider if the charges related to certain events and men, the ladies employed to wait upon her could record what was said and convey information to Kingston, who in turn relayed Anne's words to Cromwell. At some point, the charge of treason was added to the charges of adultery and incest.

On 12th May 1536, Thomas Boleyn was a member of the special commission of oyer and terminer that found Sir Henry Norris, Sir Francis Weston, William Brereton and Mark Smeaton guilty of high treason for sleeping with his daughter, the queen, and plotting with her to kill the king.[92] Thomas would have had no choice but to sit in judgement on the men and would have known that the sentence would prejudice the trial of his daughter. Thomas would have recognised that his lone dissenting voice would have paled into significance to the otherwise hostile jury who were keenly aware of their duty to the king in cases of high treason: they were merely acting as signatories to Henry's orders.

---

89 Bruce & Perowne (1853), p. 59.

90 Cavendish (1825), Vol II, p. 217.

91 L&P X. 669.

92 L&P X. 848.

Anne and George were tried separately in the King's Hall at the Tower of London on 15th May 1536. Although they defended themselves admirably, and no witnesses were produced against them, they too were found guilty of high treason and, like the other four, were sentenced to death. Their own uncle, the Duke of Norfolk, pronounced sentence as Lord High Steward, albeit weeping as he said the words.

George Boleyn went to the block with Norris, Weston, Brereton and Smeaton on 17th May 1536. Thomas Wyatt, who had also been arrested but not charged, witnessed the carnage on Tower Hill that day from his cell in the Bell Tower. He wrote that: "…these bloody days have broken my heart". Anne's execution was postponed on 18th May, which brought her grief, but Sir William Kingston reported to Cromwell her composure in her final hours, commenting that "this lady has much joy and pleasure in death."

Anne's last walk on the morning of 19th May 1536 would have taken her from the queen's lodgings, past the jewel house, where Henry had introduced her to the royal regalia, and the great hall, where she had dined the night before her coronation and where more recently her uncle had sentenced her to death. Dressed in the English fashion, complete with gable hood, Anne was led to a newly erected scaffold to the north of the White Tower. Draped in black material, it had been built to the specifications decided by Henry in the days after her arrest. Anne's husband had been particularly concerned by the minutiae of what was to happen to Anne. Standing amongst the officials on the scaffold was a swordsman employed from Calais before Anne had even set foot in a courtroom. After addressing the crowd and paying the executioner, Anne knelt upright on a bed of straw and was blindfolded. She prayed: "O Lord have mercy on me, to God I commend my soul. To Jesus Christ I commend my soul; Lord Jesu receive my soul." A single cannon fired as Anne's head was severed from her body with a single stroke of the double-handed sword. The 'Thousand Days' were over. The Boleyn siblings were laid to rest in the Chapel of St Peter ad Vincula.

The journey that Thomas and Elizabeth took from London, back to their castle of Hever during the last horrific days of Anne's queenship, was most likely full of grief and fear. There was simply nothing that Thomas and Elizabeth could do to help their children. The law had condemned both siblings and, as their parents left London, they did so with the knowledge

that their children would die. Returning to their little family manor would undoubtedly have been a painful affair. The memories of their vibrant children must have been bleeding from the walls of every chamber. Their downfall had happened so swiftly that it is possible that either or both parents were in a state of shock. Surviving today, but hidden from public view, are the original beams of the crown post roof that sat above the Boleyns' solar at Hever, and it is easy to imagine Thomas gazing into those same wooden beams, bewildered, as the reality of what had happened came crashing home. George had been Thomas's pride and his only surviving male heir, and Anne had been his joy and had brought greater wealth and power to the Boleyn family than Thomas could possibly have aspired to. Anne's rise had been unthinkable and her end unspeakable. Thomas had estates to maintain and duties to attend to, but the grief of the loss of his children changed him.

For Thomas, Hever was a place to grieve with his wife, Elizabeth, and his mother, Lady Margaret Boleyn, who had been suffering from some kind of dementia since 1519 and had moved in with the family. In June 1536, Thomas was deprived of his office of Lord Privy Seal in favour of the man who had overseen the case against his children, Thomas Cromwell.[93] In July 1536, Thomas was at Hever when he received letters from Cromwell regarding his widowed daughter-in-law Jane's financial situation. Thomas claimed that he was ill and explained that his income had been greatly reduced, but he agreed to increase Jane's allowance and death benefit.[94] Cromwell continued to harass the grieving man over the next year regarding legal subsidies and rents.

Apart from a visit to court in July 1536, when he was present in the Star Chamber at Westminster for "an assay of silver", Thomas chose to stay at Hever.[95] He may have been grieving and ill, but he needed to prove his family's loyalty to the king in light of the events of spring 1536. In October 1536, he mobilised a force to support the king during the northern Pilgrimage of Grace rebellion, and in May 1537, he served on the commission that arraigned several of the northern rebels. Five months later, he attended the christening of the new prince,

93 Wriothesley (1875), Volume I, p. 49.

94 L&P XI, 17.

95 Ibid., 45.

The Boleyn Arms in Hever's Great Hall.

Edward, bearing "a taper of virgin wax… in a towel about his neck."[96] This surely must have been a bittersweet event, for although he was celebrating the birth of a son borne by Anne's replacement, Jane Seymour, he would also have seen his granddaughter, Elizabeth, who bore the chrisom, with the help of Thomas Seymour.[97] He was still at court for the procession and burial of Queen Jane Seymour in November 1537, assisting "about the corpse and chair".[98]

Thomas probably returned to Hever in November 1538, before returning to court for New Year, when he received 20s. from the king and presented the infant Prince Edward with a gift.[99] In February 1538, Piers Butler was restored to the earldom of Ormond, with Thomas retaining the title for use in England. Thomas was to suffer a further blow in 1538, with the death of his wife, Elizabeth, on 3rd April. Elizabeth was staying at the Abbot of Reading's home near Baynard's Castle in London at the time and so was buried in St Mary's Church, Lambeth, the resting place of many other Howard women. Following Elizabeth's death, it was rumoured that Thomas would marry Lady Margaret Douglas, the king's niece, but there is no evidence of any negotiations for this match.[100]

In January 1539, Thomas was once again recorded as presenting Prince Edward with a gift, but Thomas's health was failing by this time. Of the many properties that Thomas had inherited and amassed, it was at Hever that Thomas spent his final days, dying at the castle on 12th March 1539. Robert Cranewell, Thomas's trusted steward at Hever, penned a brief note to Cromwell: "My good lord and master is dead. He departed this transitory world I trust to the everlasting Lorde, for he made the end of a good Christian man, ever remembering the goodness of Christ".[101] The Archbishop of Canterbury, Thomas Cranmer, the Boleyns' former chaplain, hastened to Hever Castle to remove Thomas's personal belongings. It proved to be an astute

---

96 Strype (1822), p. 6.
97 L&P XII, ii, 911, p. 319.
98 L&P XII, ii, 1060, p. 373.
99 L&P XIII, 5.
100 *Ibid.*, 1419.
101 L&P XIV, i, 551.

move on Cranmer's part, for within two weeks, Thomas Cromwell had sent his men to dispose of Thomas's goods.[102]

The following month, the king paid 16l. 13s. 4d. to his chaplain, William Franklyn, Dean of Windsor, "for certain oraisons, suffrages and masses to be said for the soul's health of th'erle of Wilts, late deceased", which is hard evidence that Thomas was back in favour at his death.[103] Thomas was laid to rest at Hever's Church of St Peter, where his tomb is topped by a magnificent memorial brass depicting Thomas dressed in the full robes and insignia of a Knight of the Garter, including the badge on his left breast and garter around his left knee. His head rests on a helmet surmounted by his daughter Anne Boleyn's falcon badge, and his feet rest on a griffin.

Thomas had died knowing that he would most likely be the last Boleyn to sit at Hever Castle. Much of the property Thomas had inherited from his father, including Hever, was passed to his younger brother, Sir James Boleyn. James had served his niece, Queen Anne Boleyn, as chancellor, but had survived her fall, although he chose to focus on local matters in Norfolk from then on. In February 1540, he was granted the livery of Thomas's properties. Then, in March 1540, he came to an arrangement with the king, exchanging his brother's former properties in Kent, including Hever Castle, for six manors and land in Norfolk.[104] Hever Castle was now Crown property.

102 L&P XIV, i, 608 & 609.
103 L&P XIV, 950.
104 L&P XV, 436 (40).

Lady Margaret Boleyn, who was still living in the castle at Thomas's death, had to be relocated due to her illness. She died sometime between 30th September 1539, when a sanity inquest held at Canterbury ruled that she was incompetent to handle her affairs, and 20th March 1540, when Mary Boleyn and her second husband, William Stafford, were granted livery of Margaret's lands.[105] Margaret had been the last Boleyn to reside at Hever Castle. It took until May 1543 for the Staffords to finally come into possession of Mary's inheritance, including lands at Hever, which Thomas had specified for Mary, suggesting that Thomas and Mary had reached a reconciliation in the years after the downfall of her siblings. Mary was the last of the Boleyns of Hever Castle to die, passing away just two months later, on 19th July 1543. Mary had been something of a rebel who rejected fame and wealth in favour of love. She died in relative obscurity, a wealthy woman.

105 *Ibid.*, 611 (23); Exchequer Inquisitions Post Mortem, Series II, 22 April 1539 – 21 April 1540, E 150: 87/6.

Thomas Boleyn as depicted on the memorial brass on his tomb in St Peter's Church, Hever.
NEXT PAGE: Hever's Portrait of Queen Elizabeth I, 16th century.

The Afterlife of the Boleyns of Hever Castle

The Boleyn Queen

ON 17TH November 1558, a twenty-five-year-old woman with Boleyn blood became Queen of England.

Elizabeth I is known to history as Gloriana, the Virgin Queen and Good Queen Bess. Many people worldwide recognise her portrait, yet her journey to the throne was not an easy one, and some of her contemporaries knew her as the bastard daughter of the Boleyn 'whore'. Elizabeth was the Boleyn Queen and heir.

Actress Genevieve Bujold, who played the imprisoned Anne Boleyn in "Anne of the Thousand Days", a movie filmed in part at Hever Castle, spoke these impassioned words to Richard Burton as Henry VIII: "Elizabeth shall be a greater queen than any king of yours! She shall rule a greater England than you could ever have built! Yes – MY Elizabeth SHALL BE QUEEN! And my blood will have been well spent!" The historical Anne Boleyn never saw Henry VIII again after the May Day joust of 1536. Although she appears to have met with her chaplain, Matthew Parker, and extracted a promise from him regarding Elizabeth, she could not have anticipated that her daughter would ever rule England. That marvellous piece of film was a sugar-coated fantasy that so brilliantly encapsulated the irony of Anne's daughter proving to be the greatest of Henry's heirs. Her journey to the throne would prove to be a perilous one.

After her mother's execution, an act of Parliament ruled Elizabeth illegitimate and removed her from the line of succession. She went from pampered princess to "Lady" and was sadly neglected, so much so that her governess, Lady Bryan, had to write to the king to plead for new clothes for the growing girl. It wasn't until 1546, when she was in her thirteenth year, that Elizabeth moved to court to join her stepmother Catherine Parr's household, a household that also included her half-sister, Mary. It is tempting to wonder if Elizabeth could have visited her second stepmother, Anne of Cleves, when she occupied Hever in the early years of Elizabeth's life. We certainly know the two maintained a close relationship. Several extant pieces of correspondence from Anne of Cleves, written from Hever Castle, suggest that she occupied the castle far more than historians had previously anticipated.[106]

In December 1546, Elizabeth and Mary were placed back in the line of succession, but Henry VIII did not change their status; they were still illegitimate. Just weeks later, on 28th January 1547, Henry VIII died at Whitehall, and Elizabeth's nine-year-old half-brother became King Edward VI, with his uncle, Edward Seymour, Earl of Hertford, leading his government as Lord Protector. Elizabeth soon received a proposal of marriage. Her suitor was a man twenty-five years her senior, Thomas Seymour, the king's other uncle. Elizabeth rebuffed him politely, excusing herself on the grounds that she needed to mourn her father for at least two years. The ambitious Seymour rekindled his romance with Catherine Parr, the dowager queen, and married her in secret just a few days after Elizabeth turned him down.

Elizabeth went to live with her beloved stepmother, and it wasn't long before Seymour moved in. His time in the household at Chelsea and Hanworth severely damaged Elizabeth's reputation. Later testimonies, given by Elizabeth's servants, Katherine Ashley and Thomas Parry, under interrogation at Seymour's downfall in 1549, told a tale of what we today would view as sexual abuse. Seymour would visit Elizabeth's chamber early in the morning before she was dressed and ready, and sometimes while she was still in bed. He would "strike her upon the back or on the buttocks familiarly" and tickle her, and, on occasion, he would come "in his night-gown, barelegged in his slippers". Even more disturbing was an event at Hanworth. Catherine

106 See Calendar of State Papers Domestic: Edward VI, Mary and Elizabeth, 1547-80, Queen Mary - Volume 4: August 1554, p. 63 and Thiemann, A, 'Anne of Cleves: The Queen of the Lower Rhine', Unpublished Thesis, Hever Castle Archives.

Miniature of Queen Anne of Cleves.

Parr restrained Elizabeth in the gardens there while Seymour "cut her gown in a hundred pieces". Catherine thankfully saw sense after catching her husband and stepdaughter in an embrace, and sent the girl to the home of Sir Anthony Denny. The pregnant Catherine retired to Sudeley Castle in Gloucestershire to prepare for the birth of her baby.

Elizabeth had an awful time that summer, suffering from migraines, irregular menstrual periods, digestive problems, jaundice, and anxiety attacks. She did, however, manage to mend her relationship with her stepmother, corresponding with her. She would never see Catherine again, though, for Catherine died of puerperal fever in September 1548. The ambitious Seymour was arrested in January 1549, accused of trying to kidnap the king, plotting to marry Elizabeth, and attempting to put her on the throne. He was executed on 20th March 1549 after being found guilty of 33 counts of treason.

Early 1549 was another difficult time for Elizabeth. She had to address rumours that she had been pregnant with Seymour's child, and was kept under house arrest while investigations were underway concerning whether Elizabeth was involved with her governess, Katherine Ashley, and her cofferer, Thomas Parry, in a plot with Thomas Seymour. Thankfully, while the testimonies of Ashley and Parry told a scandalous story, they did not provide evidence that Elizabeth and Seymour were planning to marry and take the throne. Ashley and Parry both stated that the princess had refused Seymour. Despite the pressure the fifteen-year-old princess was under, she did not implicate herself, and survived the scandal.

An even more stressful period in Elizabeth's youth was a few months after her half-sister, Mary, became queen. Mary I's reign brought religious changes, with Mary repealing Edward VI's religious measures and returning the country to the Catholic fold. Mary was also planning to marry the Catholic Philip of Spain, son of the Holy Emperor. A group of disaffected men began planning an uprising to remove Mary and to replace her with Elizabeth, who, they thought, could marry Edward Courtenay, Earl of Devon. Unfortunately for the conspirators, the queen's privy council got wind of trouble brewing. The rebellion, led by Sir Thomas Wyatt the Younger, son of Anne Boleyn's former admirer, poet Sir Thomas Wyatt the Elder, failed.

It is not known how much Elizabeth knew of the plot, but she was arrested and taken to the Tower of London on 18th March 1554. There, she was kept in the very same apartments in which her mother had spent her final days in 1536, while Mary I's council tried desperately to implicate her in the rebellion. Elizabeth kept her wits about her and pleaded her innocence, and Wyatt went to his death on 11th April 1554, proclaiming her innocence. For a time, Henry VIII's surviving former queen, Anne of Cleves, was suspected of involvement in the rebellion because of her proximity to Allington Castle at her home of Hever Castle. Neither Elizabeth nor Anne of Cleves was proven to have any involvement, but Anne was never again welcomed into Mary's close court in the way she had become accustomed. Elizabeth was finally released from the Tower on 19th May 1554, the anniversary of Anne Boleyn's execution. She was kept under house arrest until April 1555, when she was summoned to court to attend her half-sister during her pregnancy. The baby never came; Mary was not pregnant, so Elizabeth was given her freedom in October 1555 and allowed to travel to her estate at Hatfield.

Elizabeth was at Hatfield on 17th November 1558 when she succeeded Mary as queen. According to tradition, Elizabeth was sitting under an oak tree in the parkland around Hatfield when she received news of Mary's death. Sir Robert Naunton recorded how she fell to her knees and, "after a good time of respiration", uttered part of Psalm 18, the Latin verse translating to "this is the Lord's doing; it is marvellous in our eyes". At her coronation procession on 14th January 1559, Elizabeth paid tribute to her mother by using a vignette of Anne Boleyn as queen on the processional route. An effigy of a crowned Anne Boleyn was perhaps the most public and most full representation of Anne Boleyn that had been seen in twenty-three years. Elizabeth was crowned queen at Westminster Abbey the following day, in the same place and seat, and with the same crown that had been afforded to Anne nearly twenty-six years earlier.

Elizabeth I, daughter of Anne Boleyn, granddaughter of Thomas Boleyn, and great-great-granddaughter of Sir Geoffrey Boleyn, the man who had purchased Hever Castle back in 1462, reigned until her death on 24th March 1603. Her achievements as queen included defeating the Spanish Armada and turning England into a strong and dominant naval power, expanding England overseas through colonisation, and founding the Church of England through her religious settlement. Sadly, she also increasingly persecuted those of the Catholic faith, and her intolerance touched the walls of Hever Castle, once her mother's childhood home.

After the death of Anne of Cleves, who had been allowed to occupy Hever for seventeen years, with her rent paid for by the Crown, Mary I sold the property to one of her household favourites, Sir Edward Waldegrave. Waldegrave had been a Catholic recusant during the reign of Henry's only surviving male heir, King Edward VI. Having been imprisoned in the Tower, he was welcomed back into the royal council when Mary I came to the throne in 1553. During the early years of Elizabeth's reign, the 'Waldegrave conspiracy' saw Sir Edward and his wife back in a Tower cell.[107] There, Waldegrave died; the Tower claiming its fourth victim from the families who called Hever 'home'.

Elizabeth's reign was defined by the religious turmoil that had, in part, been set in motion when Anne Boleyn said 'yes' to Henry VIII that Christmas at Hever Castle in 1526. It was also enriched by Elizabeth's role as a patron of Science and the Arts. Her reign is known as a Golden Age, and she is by far the most famous of the Tudor monarchs. Contrary to popular belief, Elizabeth did not shy away from her disgraced mother's memory; rather, she imbued her court with her mother's emblems and motifs. Her courtiers filled their long galleries with posthumously created portraits of Anne to acknowledge the new light in which Anne was to be seen: the mother of the queen regnant. Historian Lauren Mackay draws our attention to Elizabeth's visit to Norwich Cathedral in 1578 when on progress to East Anglia. When Elizabeth entered the cathedral, full of the tombs of her Boleyn ancestors, she quietly asked that her throne be moved to face the Boleyn chapel.[108] It was a touching and public acknowledgement of her heritage. Elizabeth may have been "the lion's cub", but she was also, heart and stomach, a Boleyn.

---

107 ed. Bindoff (1982), p. 535.

108 Cited in Mackay (2018), p. 225.

Hever Castle's portrait of Queen Elizabeth I by Bettes, 16th century

Afterlife

AFTER THE tragic death of Sir Edward Waldegrave in 1561, Hever remained part of the Waldegrave estate for 150 years. The Waldegraves, like the families who would own Hever after them, chose not to live in the increasingly antiquated manor house. Rather, it was rented out to tenant farmers for income. Working tenants were far less likely to make substantial alterations to the property, which is why so much of the Boleyns' house survives today. The panelling may have changed over the years, but despite four major periods of restoration, you are very much occupying the same spaces today that the Boleyns would have known five hundred years ago.[109] The great beams that carried the often-heavy weight of history are still in situ for you to stand upon today. Eric Ives, the late great biographer of Anne Boleyn, called Hever a "fairy-tale castle" and a "romantic shrine" to Anne's relationship with Henry VIII.[110] Hever is a remarkable survivor, and in many ways, the Boleyns of Hever never left their dinky little castle, for they have long been represented and remembered there. As Cassell noted in his study of Hever in 1876, "the fair and ill-fated Anne is the dominant figure, which always fills the mind's eye when we think of her dear old home".[111]

When you walk the corridors of Hever Castle today and explore the ancient chambers with exquisitely carved panelling, you are constantly reminded of Anne Boleyn. She appears to be in the very fabric of the building, with her arms and emblems emblazoned in stained glass and

---

109 During the 1540 – 1550s, Anne of Cleves added an entrance hall to the castle and enclosed the roof of the great hall, building up the exterior walls to create a long gallery. Jane Waldo completed renovations to the castle in the 1830s, and much of the Victorian panelling she installed was removed by Captain Guy Sebright when he remodelled the castle in the 1890s. William Waldorf Astor restored the castle between 1903-08 to the standard it remains in today, preserving many of the castle's original features.

110 Ives (2004), p.3.

111 Cassell (1876), p. 19.

on the stone above fireplaces. Stunning portraits of her hang on many of its walls. You can stand before the illuminated pages of some of her most beloved books, which are both signed and inscribed by Anne before she became queen, and they were likely with her here at Hever. You can even see the initials 'AB' carved on the wall of the vice staircase of the keep, with a crudely carved axe head added between Anne's initials. As Natalie Grueninger and Sarah Morris so brilliantly stated, we are separated only by time, and not space, when we visit Hever, for we are walking in the rooms in which she thrived, and amongst her most beloved surviving possessions.[112] Like the 'ghost' of that great literary character Rebecca de Winter – also murdered by her husband – at Manderley, Anne is found everywhere at Hever. However, not all these artefacts and emblems would have been known to Anne or indeed are as authentic as they appear. Rather, they illustrate how Anne Boleyn has been remembered at Hever in the many years since she died.

The history of how these constant reminders of Anne Boleyn came to be placed at Hever is, in many ways, the history of how differently Anne Boleyn's story has been understood across the centuries. There are layers of Anne on display at Hever. By peeling back the layers of how Anne has been represented and remembered here, we may not even get any closer to the real Anne Boleyn. However, these layers can help us to understand how previous generations shaped ideas of Anne and uncover the role Hever played in moulding those understandings

Hever's impressive collection of contemporary Tudor portraiture includes four portraits labelled Anne Boleyn, one from each century since her death. An iconic sixteenth-century panel portrait of Anne Boleyn – known as the 'Hever Rose' portrait - is Anne as her daughter's generation saw her, for no known contemporary painting of Anne survives.[113] It is closely related

112 Morris & Grueninger (2013), p. 10.

113 Although no known *painted* portrait has thus far been scientifically dated to Anne's lifetime, an undisputed image of Anne Boleyn exists in the form of 'The Moost Happi' medal, struck in 1534 and which survives in the British Museum collection. Similarly, a crude sketch of Anne in the table plan for her coronation banquet in 1533, that survives in the British Library, was created in her lifetime, but it gives little detail. Two disputed Holbein sketches also exist, for which there is little solid consensus amongst art historians.

to a roundel seventeenth-century oil painting on copper, showing Anne again with her now-iconic 'B' necklace. A rosy and more youthful eighteenth-century derivative of this portrait pattern has hung for some time in the room now known as Anne Boleyn's Bedroom.

The most contentious portrait of Anne Boleyn at Hever, which divides opinion between historians, is the one held longest in the current collection and dates to the early nineteenth century. It is derivative of a disputed Holbein sketch, which remains without inscription as to the sitter's identity. The portrait hangs in Hever's inner hall, alongside a sister portrait of Mary Boleyn. The portrait of Mary was recently confirmed to be a likeness through analysis of an earlier example of this portrait in the Royal Collection.[114]

These portraits haven't always hung at Hever; rather, they have been purchased to help tell Anne's story. The twin sister portraits of Anne and Mary once hung at Warwick Castle and were purchased by William Waldorf Astor in the early 1900s.[115] The tradition of having a portrait of Anne at Hever is a long one, however, and one of the earlier references to a portrait of Anne at Hever was made by Samuel Ireland, writing in 1793. He noted a portrait of Anne in "the apartment in which she slept in [which] retains her name. Several letters of the amorous tyrant are now existing, which are addressed to her at this place".[116]

In 1823, a visitor to Hever Castle was less than impressed with the painting of Anne that he saw hanging at Hever. He wrote:

"At Hever Castle is still preserved a small picture in oil which is an heir loom, and is said to be of that queen; it is a very stiff performance, and if it is a likeness of Ann Bolen, we look in vain for those captivating charms which are generally supposed to have enslaved the affections of the despotic monarch."[117]

114 Alberge (2020).

115 Copies of these portraits still hang at Warwick Castle, in the original initialled gold frames.

116 Ireland (1793), p. 93.

117 Bell (1823), Literary Gleanings: Gleanings from ancient Lore, p. 29.

In 1801, similar feelings were expressed by another visitor to Hever who had observed a similar portrait of Anne at Rufford Abbey:

"In the attic story... a portrait of Anne Bullen on wood, but by no means as handsome as Holbein has painted her in which is preserved at Loseley in Surrey; yet as this one bears a great resemblance to a portrait of her at Hever Castle in Kent, the seat of her family, one is almost led to suspect that Henry's taste for beauty would not have been much followed at the present day."[118]

A portrait of Anne, which derives from the 'B' necklace pattern, still hangs at Loseley, so the one at Hever in 1801 likely differed from this model. Intriguingly, a portrait that is believed to have hung at Hever Castle is still owned by descendants of the Meade-Waldo family, who were then owners of the castle. Historian Alison Weir proposed that the portrait could be Anne of Cleves, who lived at Hever in the years after her annulment from King Henry VIII.[119] More intriguing still is the inscription on the painting. It reads 'Anna Regina A.D. 1534', suggesting that the individual inscribing the portrait believed it to depict Anne Boleyn, who was Queen Anne in that year. It may be that this portrait depicts neither of the queens called Anne who lived at Hever, but its presence at Hever tells us that Anne was actively remembered here.

As well as portraiture, legends were a long-lasting feature of the afterlife of Anne Boleyn. Although it is well known that Hever opened to the paying public formally in 1963, many visitors paid to experience Hever long before it opened as a business in the twentieth century, and many legends were peddled to entertain paying visitors. One of the earliest recorded examples that we have of a Hever legend about Anne is from the late 1790s, when it was stated that Anne Boleyn had been spared the sword and had, instead, died in a dungeon at Hever. Later iterations of this story conceded that she had died by the sword at the Tower but that she had been held prisoner at Hever before her untimely end.[120] Notwithstanding that Hever never had any dungeons, it appears that the Boleyns' parlour was once nicknamed 'the dungeon' in the eighteenth century

118 Hodgson, John and F. C. Laird (1813), p. 390.

119 Weir (2015).

120 Burr (1766), p. 188; Knight (1850), Vol III, p. 4.

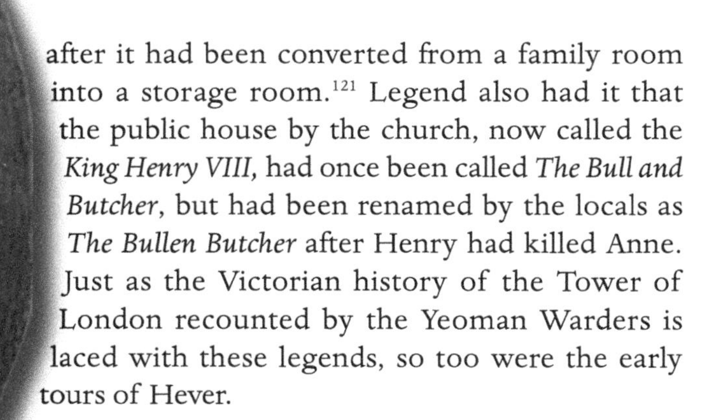

after it had been converted from a family room into a storage room.[121] Legend also had it that the public house by the church, now called the *King Henry VIII*, had once been called *The Bull and Butcher*, but had been renamed by the locals as *The Bullen Butcher* after Henry had killed Anne. Just as the Victorian history of the Tower of London recounted by the Yeoman Warders is laced with these legends, so too were the early tours of Hever.

Hever would be open on specified dates, and the public would be allowed to see the principal rooms of the former Boleyn house. It was not long before royalty was once again at Hever. On the afternoon of Saturday 13th September 1834, Princess Alexandrina Victoria – later Queen Victoria - journeyed from Tonbridge Wells to Hever Castle. She wrote in her diary that evening that:

"At a quarter past 1 we drove with Lady Flora and dear Lehzen to Hever Castle. We arrived there at 3. This curious old place was the residence of Sir Thomas Boleyn, father of poor Queen Anne Boleyn. We saw the room where she used to live and sat on a seat on which Henry VIII used to sit. We then mounted our horses. Mr Conroy met us there. I rode Rosa."[122]

Victoria seemed to be captivated by Anne's story and would later paint and draw many pictures of Anne Boleyn, such as a dramatic scene from Donizetti's opera, with Anne pleading

---

121 There were two trap doors in the long gallery, one of which led to the room which had formerly been the Boleyn's parlour.

122 Queen Victoria's Journals, Volume: 5 (20th May 1834 - 4th November 1834).

A miniature of Anne Boleyn.

with Henry for her life.[123] When she was queen, Victoria purchased several items believed to be the possessions of Anne, such as the marriage clock gifted to Anne by Henry, a copy of which in silver was installed at Hever from 1903.[124] She also ensured the restoration of the Tower's Chapel of St Vincula, and for the first time marking out Anne's grave. The marking of Anne's scaffold site, though inaccurate, was part of making Anne more visible at sites where her history played out. Just as the Tower of London was modified during Victoria's reign to accommodate an increased interest in Anne in popular culture, so too was the image of Anne at Hever reimagined for its Victorian audience with the addition of a faux Anne Boleyn bedchamber.

The artist Joseph Nash created two engravings of Hever Castle for his 1839 book *The Mansions of England in the Olden Time.* The first shows the castle's courtyard just after Hever's then-owner, Jane Waldo, had renovated some of the castle's interiors. You can see to the far left-hand side of the engraving that Nash has captured the long since gone door on the east elevation, which would have given access to the domestic side of the household.[125] Henry VIII is depicted arriving through the gatehouse, with a young Anne Boleyn in a gable hood watching from a window. The second engraving shows Henry VIII courting Anne Boleyn in Hever's long gallery. The gallery's original panelling can be seen in the sketch, as can the seat on which Queen Victoria had sat when visiting as a princess, which was then believed to have been the one that Henry occupied.

In 1866, a group of artists known as the 'St John's Wood Clique' rented Hever for summer sketching and painting. It was used as a backdrop for several paintings set in the Tudor era, many of which drew upon stories about Anne. David Wilkie Winfield painted a dramatic scene of Anne being arrested at Greenwich Palace, later remodelling sketches of Hever's great hall as a backdrop. He also painted a more solemn scene with angels visiting Anne in her bedchamber before her execution, which he set in the so-called 'Anne Boleyn Bedchamber' at Hever. William

123 See 'Scene from Anna Bolena c. 1837 - c. 1841', [https://www.rct.uk/collection/980019-am]

124 See 'Anne Boleyn Clock 1530-1870?', [https://www.rct.uk/collection/search#/4/collection/30018/anne-boleyn-clock]

125 This door would have led to the buttery, larder and kitchens during the Boleyns' tenure.

NEXT PAGE: Anne Boleyn's Bedroom by William Frederick Yeames, c.1866.

Frederic Yeames created a painting of a 'ghost hunt' in the bedroom traditionally believed to be Anne's. It shows the room with its original larger proportions, accommodating a four-poster bed with yellow curtains and showing the entrance to the peephole window to the great hall.

William Waldorf Astor was also a devotee to Anne Boleyn's story, and he was already amassing items relating to her life before he secured the purchase of Hever Castle in 1903. Perhaps no other individual has brought more of Anne back to Hever than he. Among hundreds of other contemporary Early Modern artefacts, he purchased two prayer books that had belonged to Anne: the 1527/8 Book of Hours and a small psalter. He also purchased a prayer book illustrated by the celebrated court artist Nicholas Hilliard for Queen Elizabeth I.[126] Astor's architect, Frank Loughborough Pearson, oversaw the insertion of Tudor and Boleyn emblems throughout the plasterwork ceilings and the carved panelling he lavished on the somewhat dishevelled Boleyn home. A balcony was added to the Boleyn's former kitchens, and the design was drawn from the rood screen at King's College Chapel, Cambridge, installed by Henry VIII for Anne. Anne's white falcon emblem returned to Hever when Clayton and Bell, the renowned stained-glass manufacturers, installed the heraldic arms of the Boleyns in Hever's long gallery. The initials 'AB' and 'HR' were added in shields along the

126 Anne Boleyn's girdle Psalter and Elizabeth's Prayer Book illustrated by Hilliard were stolen from Hever in a large robbery in 1946.

Henry VIII arriving at Hever Castle by Joseph Nash, c.1839.

length of that glorious room's plasterwork ceiling, and Tudor roses were added to that found in the room formerly the Boleyns' kitchen. Anne had never been so present in Hever's décor.

William Waldorf Astor's fascination with Anne gave him respect for the house he inherited, and he saved as much of the original fabric of the house as possible. Astor's Hever was a far more private one than had been the case in the previous century, and his curation of the rooms provided the ultimate after-dinner tour for the many auspicious guests who would come to stay. From Winston Churchill to Queen Elizabeth II and Prince Philip, some of the most powerful and renowned figures of the twentieth century have experienced Hever's charm. John Jacob Astor V, William's son, was more than candid about some of the less authentic additions to the castle by his father. When asked if Henry VIII had slept in the

Henry VIII with Anne Boleyn in the Long Gallery by Joseph Nash, c.1839.

chamber named after that king, he replied that the only king to have slept in the said room was 'Rex' Harrison.[127]

Harrison had played Henry VIII in the premiere run of Maxwell Anderson's popular play *Anne of the Thousand Days* in 1948. While Anderson's early post-war Anne Boleyn was fiery, Anderson's play was really about Henry VIII, despite the promise in the glorious title. As Susan Bordo revealed in her landmark study of Anne Boleyn's 'creation', King Henry VIII was originally given the final words in the play.[128] Haunted by his actions in killing Anne, he cries that he will look "...forever down the long corridors of air, finding them empty, hearing only echoes... It would have been easier to forget you living than to forget you dead."[129] The play's frank discussion of adultery and incest prevented film adaptation until the late 1960s, when the restrictive Hollywood's 'Hayes' code was lifted.[130] However, the film version changed Anderson's play and made it all about Anne.

Hal B Wallis, who had produced the 1964 film *Becket* with actor Richard Burton, produced the film version of *Anne of the Thousand Days* with Burton cast as Henry. Elizabeth Taylor had wished to play the role of Anne, but the part was given to the French-Canadian Genevieve Bujold, who forever changed the face of Anne Boleyn on screen. Wallis secured the rights with Gavin Astor, John Jacob's son, to film much of Anne's story at Hever Castle. In the late 1960s screenplay by Bridget Boland and John Hale, it is Anne who speaks the last lines: an echo of the defiant, furious, and forgivably fictitious 'Tower' scene. Bujold's Anne shredded Burton's Henry by prophesying that the son and heir he had 'ripped and torn the body of the church and his friends' to secure would be overshadowed by her Boleyn heir: Elizabeth. It is a glorious scene

127 It is likely that the rooms located on the east elevation (where the King Henry VIII bedchamber is) were used for servants during the Boleyns' tenure, as there were no fireplaces in these rooms before William Waldorf Astor's renovations.

128 Bordo (2013), p. 188.

129 Stephanie Russo discusses this scene in Russo, S. (2020), p. 168.

130 Bordo (2013), p. 181.

The balcony in Hever's inner hall, inspired by the rood screen at King's College Chapel, Cambridge.

that allows us to feel that Anne went down fighting and with a confident belief in her daughter's future succession; that her "blood" was indeed "well spent".

In earlier films about Anne Boleyn, she was portrayed as a hunted and betrayed victim of Henry's greed, as was the case in the 1920 silent film *Anna Bolena*, which spoke closely to the Victorian model of Anne's story, which had so beguiled Queen Victoria. Audiences only saw a snippet of Anne's resilient end in the 1930 comedy romp, *The Private Life of Henry VIII*. *Anne of the Thousand Days* showed a markedly different Anne: one who is willing to oppose not only her parents - risking Hever Castle being pulled down about the Boleyns' ears - but also willing to defy the king. This is a woman who laid down the terms of her acquiescence: the crown. This Anne asked for power in return for the promise of a son and showed a queen not afraid to exercise the power given to her. It is the moment Anne Boleyn got complex and messy in popular culture.

In an interview at Hever Castle in 1968, Bujold stated of Anne Boleyn: "I love her. I have read a great deal about Anne Boleyn but now I would like to meet her. I feel I know her, so I hope I am making her as alive and 'now' as possible."[131] Interviewed many years later by Susan Bordo, Bujold was asked if she wanted to see a particular actor play her in the future, to which she spiritedly replied: "No: Anne is mine."[132] In many ways, Bujold is right. Anne Boleyn was never again put back into the passive and more comfortable box in which the Victorians had so dearly observed her. This was a brave, bold and defiant Anne, reflective of the political landscape of the late 1960s. In many ways, every on-screen Anne since has their roots in Bujold's watershed performance.

The fact that nearly a third of the film was shot at Hever Castle imbued it with a sense of authenticity that masks many of its historical inaccuracies. It drew in huge crowds to Hever: a much-needed boost to the dwindling funds of the Astor family, who had in 1968 endured the second disastrous flooding of the castle in 10 years. Hal B Wallis gifted the Astors one of the Tudor-style prop tents that had been erected by the film crew on Anne Boleyn's orchard, and it was used to serve tea to the burgeoning visitors who had taken Bujold's Anne to heart. Costume

131 'Anne of a Thousand Days, 1960's - Film 227'.

132 Bordo (2013), p. 196.

Genevieve Bujold as Anne Boleyn at Hever Castle in the 1969 film "Anne of the Thousand Days".

designer Margaret Furse had even replicated the clothing worn in Hever's portrait labelled Anne after Holbein, and that image became the dominant one in Hever guidebooks and on souvenirs.

When the Astor Family finally sold Hever Castle in 1983, the Guthrie Family carried on the tradition of investing in items relating to Anne Boleyn and her contemporaries at the Tudor court. They have now amassed such a vast and culturally important collection that the celebrated art historian Philip Mould has dubbed it "the greatest privately owned public collection of portraits that tells the story of the Tudors." Historian Kate Williams called Hever a "Tudor Time Machine", and it is easy to see why so many esteemed historians have chosen to film influential and popular documentaries about Anne and the Tudors here. Lucy Worsley, Tracy Borman and Suzannah Lipscomb are amongst the many celebrated historians who have chosen Hever as a location to illustrate to a wide audience its important and ever-popular history.

Hever Castle is emblematic of the many achievements of the Boleyns. In just three generations, the Boleyns had ensured that Anne and her siblings had a privileged education and refined upbringing. Hever is the only surviving witness to some of the most remarkable annals in our history. The Boleyns of Hever's many extraordinary successes ensured that Hever was a place where astonishing history happened. Everything changed when Anne said "yes" to Henry VIII. Future generations will explore different versions of Anne's story, and undoubtedly Hever will incorporate new ideas and fresh evidence into their experience in the decades ahead. What seems almost certain is that while the picture-postcard castle stands, as it has for well over 600 years, Hever Castle and the ever-dazzling Boleyn family will remain indelibly linked in the popular consciousness.

Hever Castle's portrait of Anne Boleyn, 17th century.

An Insider's Guide to Hever Castle Today

HEVER CASTLE itself is a remarkable surviving witness to the astounding story of the Boleyn family. While some of Hever's interiors are cosmetically distinct from their original usage, the castle's exterior has barely changed since the Boleyns' time. The whitewash, which hid the Tudor brickwork of some of the Boleyns' additions to the castle, has faded away over time, revealing the beautiful sandstone of the hewn blocks which make up the curtain walls and the keep. Still hanging in place, over 600 years later, is the original portcullis under which many important heads passed. The house may be larger now than the one occupied by its most famous residents, but internally it contains the bones and heart of the Boleyns' manor, which generations since have fleshed out into a living museum of their significance. Its current owners, the Guthrie family, have played a vital role in continuing to furnish Hever with artefacts closely related to their story, while delicately retaining those important layers of the Boleyn story that tell us so much about how they were viewed in the centuries after their glory days.

When we visit Hever Castle, we walk in the Boleyns' celebrated footsteps, and we can view the sites and objects they loved. Surviving palaces like Hampton Court and the Tower of London can transport us to the glory days of the Boleyns' rise to power and the most tragic moments of their fall. However, the queen's lodgings and the privy apartments at both important sites have long since gone. Similarly, much of Anne's ancestral home at Blickling was reimagined in 1616. Although many of Hever's chambers were afforded an exquisite veneer of Tudor-style panelling and plasterwork by William Waldorf Astor, the wall plates, braces, and purlins that make up the timbered structure of the Boleyns' house remain for us to enjoy today. New items will be added to the collection over time, and existing ones may be presented to visitors in different areas of the castle. This is an insider's guide to some of what we consider to be the must-see items of the remarkable Hever Castle collection as it exists today.

Hever Castle's inner hall, the first room on the current visitor's route, was created in the space once occupied by the Boleyns' kitchens. Evidence suggests that the kitchens were moved to the great hall when the chimney to the fireplaces collapsed in the nineteenth century, and then moved by Guy Sebright - who rented the castle in the 1890s - to the rear of the castle, across the moat. This relocation of the kitchens allowed William Waldorf Astor to reimagine this space as a greeting hall, where strong aperitifs would be served before dinner.

Astor also moved the main staircase to this space and installed a gallery for musicians to entertain his many notable guests. Frank Loughborough Pearson, Astor's architect, had travelled the country to get inspiration from extant Tudor manors and palaces for Hever's decor. The carved screen on the balcony in the inner hall was inspired by the rood screen at King's College Chapel, Cambridge, that survives today and which was created during Anne Boleyn's reign. The original is highly decorated with Anne's initials and emblems, while the later creation at Hever is a plainer homage to a key artefact of Anne's brief time as queen.

Tudor roses were added in plasterwork to the ceiling of the inner hall, in recognition of the four Tudor monarchs who owned the castle and the two queens consort who called it 'home'.[133] You can also find the silver replica of the marriage clock gifted to Anne Boleyn by King Henry VIII in this room. Many portraits now hang in this space, including a sixteenth-century portrait of King Henry VIII after the celebrated court artist, Hans Holbein the Younger. He accompanies the two eighteenth-century portraits of Anne and Mary Boleyn, also after Holbein, which hang on either side of the fully functional fireplace.

Where the Boleyns' larder and dairy were located is now a stunning drawing room, with exquisite inlaid panelling inspired from that created by Thomas Boynton in c.1575-85 at Sizergh Castle in Cumbria. Today's room is a magnificent example of how the Astor family combined historical aesthetics with Edwardian comfort, and it is the most evocative example of Astor's style.

Hever Castle's great hall has a wonderful stone-carved version of the Boleyn arms above the fireplace, installed by John Jacob Astor in recognition of their time at the castle. The original green men, carved onto the screen that Geoffrey Boleyn used to partition off a parlour, are also still visible. This room has since had a much lower ceiling installed, when a gallery was placed above it. Later still, William Waldorf Astor decorated the ceiling with timbers brought in from

---

133 The four monarchs who owned Hever Castle were King Henry VIII, King Edward VI, Queen Jane (Lady Jane Grey), and Queen Mary I, who all owned Hever as part of the Crown Estate between 1540-1557. Queen Anne Boleyn and Queen Anne of Cleves were the queens consort who called it 'home'.

the Blickling estate as a nod to the Boleyns' ancestral home. The doorway to the parlour (now the morning room), which used to be located to the north of the screen, is now long gone, as are the courtyard windows to the south, which were closed when an entrance hall was added in the mid to late sixteenth century.

A room that has kept close to its original usage is Hever's library, where the offices of the Boleyns' estate would have been located. This is where the original staircase to the Boleyns' great chamber was once situated, to the room's northwest. It is now furnished with sabicu wood

King Henry VIII's personal lock in Hever's great hall, 16th century.

panelling in the style of the Anglo-Dutch carver Grinling Gibbons. A study has been partitioned off beyond the southernmost bookshelves, which were based on those once owned by the diarist Samuel Pepys.

While the drawing room and library have a distinct Edwardian touch, the morning room - once known as the Boleyns' Parlour – has a far older feel. Despite its current name, this is very much an afternoon room, for as it faces northwest, it does not enjoy the sun until the early afternoon. As the sun goes down in the evening, the light catches the ripples from the moat, and it dances on the ceiling by the window frames, which once lit the dais of the great hall.

The vice staircase to the Boleyns' solar is intact, and it is remarkable when climbing up its winding structure to think of the many gowns that have swept up against the stone walls over the years. This staircase was later extended up to service the long gallery after the Boleyns' time. In the early days of the Astors' opening of the castle in the 1960s, visitors would continue up this way as the family still occupied the middle floor of Hever. Today, visitors alight halfway up the staircase at Anne Boleyn's bedroom, for most of the house is now open to explore.

Anne Boleyn's bedroom is a surprisingly small space, made smaller by the addition of a built-in wardrobe during the Astors' tenure. This space has a long history of being identified as Anne Boleyn's bedroom., Another eighteenth-century portrait of Anne, wearing her famous 'B' necklace, hangs in this room in recognition of that tradition. You will also see a half-domed ceiling in front of the window, an original Tudor feature that provided greater light. A wooden chest, carved with the name 'Bullen' and the word 'Hever' is also located in this space, though it is most certainly a later piece. Similarly, a bed carved with Anne Boleyn's name was long held in this bedroom, though it too is a later creation and is now on display in the 'Queen's Chamber'.

Anne Boleyn's Books of Hours are undoubtedly the stars in Hever's Boleyn collection. The beautifully illuminated manuscript, created c.1410-1450 in Bruges, contains Anne's prophetic inscription *"Le temps viendra, Je Anne Boleyn"* (The Time Will Come, I Anne Boleyn). This book was likely gifted to Anne by a female relative, as they were chiefly used by women and had intergenerational familial ownership. The later book, created in Paris c.1528, was probably created especially for Anne, and she was certainly its first owner. In it, she wrote a rhyming couplet:

"Remember me when you do pray,
That hope doth lead from day to day.
Anne Boleyn".

These books are on public display in the Boleyns' great chamber, now more commonly known as the Books of Hours Room. They are as about as close as you can get to Anne Boleyn today. One of Hever Castle's longest-serving stewards, Iain Smith, reminds Hever's visitors that Anne Boleyn's DNA is all over these treasured possessions. She has left us not only her words

Anne Boleyn's Book of Hours, c.1410-1450.

but the very essence of her faith and style, evidenced across their pages. They are the jewels in Hever Castle's impressive collection.

Also located in this room is a marriage plaque celebrating the Boleyn family's most noteworthy marriages: Thomas Boleyn to Lady Elizabeth Howard and Anne Boleyn to King Henry VIII. This wooden plaque, complete with the combined arms of these marriages, is a pre-Astor relic. Pictorial evidence survives, with a now sadly missing twin plaque, when it was located in the central chamber of the keep - the room now known as the council chamber - in the 1830s. Little is known about this plaque's creation, but it has hung at various places in the castle for many years and is one of the earlier examples of the many Boleyn-related items added to Hever. A reproduction of the memorial brass placed on the tomb of Thomas Boleyn can also be seen in his great chamber, and the original can be viewed at St Peter's Church. A printed rubbing of the brass can also be viewed in Hever Castle's gallery.

The Boleyns' great chamber would undoubtedly have been hung with fine tapestries and arras, and today it houses two significant tapestries. The armorial tapestry bears the arms of King Henry VIII and was listed in the inventories of the king's possessions taken upon his death. William Waldorf Astor purchased the other as a marriage tapestry, created in c.1525, and purported at the time of sale to depict the wedding of Princess Mary Tudor, Henry VIII's sister, to King Louis XII of France. This event was attended by Mary Boleyn, and possibly Anne. More recent attention has been paid to the word 'Esther' woven onto the bride's dress, which would suggest that this is a biblical scene evoking the story of Queen Esther. It is no less pertinent to Anne Boleyn's story for this re-evaluation. On Passion Sunday, during the final months of Anne's queenship, her almoner, John Skip, used the story of Queen Esther and her triumph over the king's wicked minister Haman in a sermon that acted as a warning shot across the bow of Thomas Cromwell, Henry VIII's minister. It was not the queen who prevailed in Anne's case, for Cromwell went on to play a crucial role in bringing the Boleyn family crashing down.

In the Boleyns' best bedchamber, now known as the 'Queen's Chamber' owing to the six portraits that purport to depict Henry's six queens, we find Hever's seventeenth-century roundel portrait of Anne Boleyn. This posthumous portrait was painted on copper and was likely created

Æ LE TEMPS V

RA ÆB
ÆB REMEMBER ME ÆB
The Books of Hours
in this room are both inscribed
and signed by Anne Boleyn.
Hours were personal prayer
books which were popular in
England from the 15th century
until the Reformation.
Short services to the Virgin
Mary were read at eight fixed
Hours during the day.
Hours also contained a
calendar of church festivals,
psalms, prayers to favourite
saints and services for the dead.
They were often made to order
with minor variations to suit
the purchaser.
These Books of Hours were
made for English owners with
English saints and prayers.

as a corridor portrait set. Philip Mould has hypothesised that it may even have been created to be set into the panelling of a long gallery.[134]

The staircase gallery, which was added shortly after the Boleyns' time at Hever, features two contemporary portraits of the Boleyn heir, Queen Elizabeth I. The first is a particularly rare example of an early portrait of Elizabeth created in the first few years of her reign. Known as the 'Chawton Portrait', for it was once owned by Jane Austen and her family at Chawton house, it shows Elizabeth before she had crafted the highly controlled, symbolic, and stylised imagery found in later models. A good example of this carefully curated imagery can be found in the second and perhaps more impressive portrait of Elizabeth, which is attributed to the Elizabethan artist John Bettes. Elizabeth controlled her later portraiture closely, and this example has a facial pattern drawn from the famous 'Darnley Portrait'. Beautifully embroidered on Elizabeth's sleeve in blackwork are the emblems of honeysuckle and acorns, which were the emblems used by Anne Boleyn and Henry VIII. The acorn was also adopted by Elizabeth's favourite, Robert Dudley.

In the so-called King Henry VIII bedchamber, which was most likely the servants' dormitory during the Boleyns' ownership, can be found an early lithograph of Hans Holbein's sketch, which was labelled as Anne Boleyn by John Cheke, tutor to Henry VIII's son, Edward, and which is held in the Royal Collection. This simple but striking sketch, which depicts a woman of high status in a nightgown, divides opinion amongst historians as to the sitter's identity.[135] Above the fireplace, added by William Waldorf Astor, can be found a elaborate carving of Henry VIII and the two of his queens who lived at Hever: Anne Boleyn to his left, and Anne of Cleves to his right. This carving of Anne Boleyn was drawn from the other disputed Holbein sketch that is often labelled as her, held in the British Museum.

---

134 Portrait of Anne Boleyn (c. 1507-36), 1600c., Anglo Flemish School, Historical Portraits Image Library. [http://www.historicalportraits.com/Gallery.asp?Page=Item&ItemID=591&Desc=Anne-Boleyn-|--Anglo-Flemish-School]

135 Grosvenor, Bendor, 'Anne Boleyn regains her head', Art History News, 15 December 2011. [https://www.arthistorynews.com/articles/894_Anne_Boleyn_regains_her_head]

Carving of Anne Boleyn in Henry VIII's Bedchamber.

Keen observers and lovers of Hever may have noticed that the impressive long gallery has been absent from our journey through the Boleyns' castle. It has long been the tradition that the castle's long gallery was where King Henry VIII held court when visiting the Boleyns at Hever. Long galleries certainly existed when Thomas Boleyn and his family arrived at Hever in 1505. As the architectural historian Rosalys Coope noted in her study of the origins of the long gallery, the example at Richmond Palace had been built c.1506, replacing an earlier example. Other examples of early long galleries in private country houses include one at Thornbury Castle, built by Edward Stafford, Duke of Buckingham, c.1511, and those created by Archbishop William Warham and Cardinal Thomas Wolsey. Moreover, we know that galleries were created especially for the visits of Henry VIII and Anne Boleyn, such as at Shurland, in the Isle of Sheppey, created in 1532.[136]

However, Coope dated Hever's long gallery, formed over the medieval great hall, to c.1584, when Charles Waldegrave had ownership of the castle. Upon inspection of the exterior stonework of the gallery, where the date of 1584 is supposed to be located, we have been unable to locate this vital clue to this feature's age. Moreover, we have no evidence that Charles used Hever Castle during his lifetime. He appears to have resided with his recusant wife, Jeronima, chiefly at their numerous properties in Norfolk. Until the ancient beams that make up the structure of this impressive gallery are tested, we will not be certain which generation of Hever's owners created it. If it were created by the Boleyns, it would be amongst the earliest examples of a long gallery above a great hall in England. If it was built after the Boleyns, which seems to be more likely, then it is possible that the alterations occurred during the period when the Crown owned the castle.

---

136 Coope, R, 'The 'Long Gallery': Its Origins, Development, Use, and Decoration' in Architectural History, Vol. 29 (1986), pp.43-67.

Anne Boleyn's initials in Hever Castle's long gallery.

For now, a tantalising question mark hovers over the creation date of this evocative space. Nevertheless, it has a long tradition of being connected to the Boleyns, and William Waldorf Astor saturated the impressive space with Anne Boleyn's initials and the arms of the Boleyns who owned the castle. It has also been furnished with one of the most significant collections of Tudor portraiture on public display today. Amongst these contemporary portraits hangs the famous 'Hever Rose Portrait' of Anne Boleyn.

The last room on the visitor's route is the 'Council Chamber', which houses a collection of torture and execution implements collected by William Waldorf Astor. It contains four beheading swords, similar to the one used to end Anne's life. One example, created in Germany in the sixteenth century, is etched with a haunting image of a woman kneeling, blindfolded, awaiting the blade, which is being held aloft by the executioner. It is a chilling reminder of what that horrific moment on 19th May 1536 would have looked like; the moment that marked the end of the Boleyns' inspiring rise to power and the beginning of the end of their time at Hever Castle.

Hever does not easily give up its secrets, yet the opaque parts of Hever's past will provide opportunities for future researchers to uncover. Our knowledge of the lives of the many people who have lived here is ever-changing, and Hever will be the beneficiary of such research for many years to come. It remains one of, if not the most evocative and rich places to experience the story of the Boleyns. Whatever has been said about the character of this famous (or infamous) family and their legacy, nobody could doubt the longevity of their prominence, and Hever Castle will remain the most redolent portal into their dazzling world.

Etching of an execution on a 16th century beheading sword.

Acknowledgements

We would like to thank the late, great Eric Ives, Adrienne Dillard, Natalie Grueninger, Sarah Morris, James Peacock, Gareth Russell, Lauren Mackay, Natalia Richards, Susan Bordo, Amy Licence, Elizabeth Norton, Tracy Borman, Suzannah Lipscomb, Clare Cherry, Julia Fox, Charlie Fenton and Sandra Vasoli for their compelling and enriching contributions to the knowledge of the Boleyn family. We stand on the shoulders of giants.

Iain Smith, one of Hever Castle's most knowledgeable stewards, has helpfully challenged and shaped the conclusions we have reached. He is an endless fount of Hever knowledge, and our research is so much richer for his valued contributions.

We would like to thank Duncan Leslie, the Guthrie family, Sarah Cole, Helen Francis, and Lisa Allen for their generous assistance with furnishing this study with such beautiful pictures of Hever and its treasures.

We would like to thank Tim Ridgway for turning our idea into reality and his technical help with images and plans.

I (Owen) would like to thank my wonderful family, Sally-Ann, Luke, Enid, Roy, Georgia, Mark, Sophia, Amelie and Lily, and my best friend Michael for their love and support, and their understanding of my long absences from their company while completing this study.

I (Claire) would like to thank my husband, Tim, for his love, support and enthusiasm for this book project, and my family, Verity, Joel, Christian, Kira and Iden, Frank and Davida Brassington, and Geoff Ridgway, for putting up with my Tudor history obsession. I would also like to say a huge thank you to Owen for being the very best co-author I could possibly work with and a good friend.

Lastly, this book would not have been possible without the help and support of Hever Castle's incomparable curator, Alison Palmer. Countless joyful hours have been spent with Alison walking through Hever's chambers and theorising how the Boleyn's house would have functioned. Alison is a highly skilled and devoted custodian of Hever's magnificent collection, and it is an honour to have gained so much knowledge from her. Hever has never been in more steadfast hands.

Dr Owen Emmerson

OWEN EMMERSON is a social and cultural historian who gained his doctorate from the University of Sussex. His doctoral thesis examined the abolition of corporal punishment.

He has contributed to several documentaries about the Tudor court and is the co-founder of the *"Inside Hever Castle"* online subscription service. He works at Hever as Castle Historian and Assistant Curator.

Claire Ridgway

CLAIRE RIDGWAY is a full-time historian specialising in Tudor history. She is the author of several Tudor history books, including *The Fall of Anne Boleyn: A Countdown*, *On This Day in Tudor History* and *George Boleyn: Tudor Poet, Courtier & Diplomat*, which she co-authored with Clare Cherry. Claire is the founder of The Anne Boleyn Files blog and Tudor Society and runs the popular Anne Boleyn Files & Tudor Society YouTube channel.

List of Illustrations

32 The arms of Geoffrey Boleyn in Hever Castle's long gallery – used with permission of Hever Castle and Gardens.

35 The original door to the screens passage, with trefoils on the spandrels – used with permission of Hever Castle and Gardens.

38 Hever Castle's great hall today – used with permission of Hever Castle and Gardens.

40 The arms of William Boleyn in Hever Castle's long gallery – used with permission of Hever Castle and Gardens.

41 The arms of Thomas Boleyn in Hever Castle's long gallery – used with permission of Hever Castle and Gardens.

42 Hever Castle's portrait of King Henry VII, 16th century – used with permission of Hever Castle and Gardens.

46 The arms of Thomas Boleyn, held in Hever's archive – used with permission of Hever Castle and Gardens.

48 Hever Castle's portrait of Prince Arthur – used with permission of Hever Castle and Gardens.

50 'Anne Boleyn's Bedroom' today – used with permission of Hever Castle and Gardens.

52 Hever Castle's portrait of Anne Boleyn, after Holbein, 18th century – used with permission of Hever Castle and Gardens.

53 Hever Castle's portrait of Mary Boleyn, after Holbein, 18th century – used with permission of Hever Castle and Gardens.

57 Hever Castle's copy of a letter from Thomas Boleyn to Margaret of Austria – used with permission of Hever Castle and Gardens.

58 Hever Castle's Wedding Tapestry, c.1525 – used with permission of Hever Castle and Gardens.

61 Miniatures of King Francis I, Marguerite of Angoulême and Queen Claude, 18th century – reproduced from the collection of Dr Owen Emmerson.

64 The north elevation of Hever Castle, 18th century watercolour – Reproduced with the kind permission of Alison Palmer, Curator of Hever Castle.

69 Hever Castle's Portrait of Anne Boleyn, 18th century – used with permission of Hever Castle and Gardens.

Bibliography

Alberge, Dalya (2020, 30 May) 'Mysterious woman in Royal Collection portrait identified as Mary Boleyn', *The Telegraph*, https://www.telegraph.co.uk/news/2020/05/30/mysterious-woman-royal-collection-portrait-identified-king-henry/.

'Anne of a Thousand Days, 1960's - Film 227', Huntley Archives, https://www.youtube.com/watch?v=YyZS0EUgpzg&t=4s.

Bell, J. (1823, January) 'Literary Gleanings: Gleanings from Ancient Lore', *La Belle Assemblée being Bell's Court and Fashionable Magazine for January 1823*. J. M. McGowan.

ed. Bindoff, S.T. (1982) *The History of Parliament: the House of Commons 1509-1558*. Secker and Warburg.

Blomefield, Francis, and Charles Parkin (1808) *An essay towards a topographical history of the county of Norfolk*, Volumes VII, VIII, IX, William Miller.

Bordo, Susan (2013) *The Creation of Anne Boleyn: A New Look at England's Most Notorious Queen*. Houghton Miffin Harcourt.

Bruce, John & Thomas Thomason Perowne (1853), eds. *The Correspondence of Matthew Parker, D.D., Archbishop of Canterbury: Comprising Letters Written by and to Him, from A.D. 1535, to His Death, A.D. 1575*. Cambridge University Press.

Bullen, Frank (2008, March), 'Anne Boleyn: A Norfolk Girl?', http://archiver.rootsweb.ancestry.com/th/read/norfolk/2008-03/1206716205.

Burr, T. B. (1766) *The History of Tunbridge Wells*, 1st ed. M. Hingeston; J. Dodsley; T. Caslon; and E. Baker.

Calendar of Letter-Books of the City of London: K, Henry VI, ed. Reginald R Sharpe (1911).

Calendar of State Papers Domestic: Edward VI, Mary and Elizabeth, 1547-80, Queen Mary - Volume 4: August 1554, ed. Robert Lemon. (1856)

Calendar of State Papers Relating To English Affairs in the Archives of Venice, Volume 4, 1527-1533, ed. Rawdon Brown (1871).

Calendar of State Papers, Spain: Further Supplement To Volumes 1 and 2, Documents From Archives in Vienna, ed. Garrett Mattingly (1947).

Calendar of State Papers, Spain, Volume 4 Part 2, 1531-1533, ed. Pascual de Gayangos (1882).

Calendar of the Fine Rolls preserved in the Public Record Office, 1485-1509. Vol. 22, Henry VII. Her Majesty's Stationery Office (1962).

Calendar of the Patent Rolls preserved in the Public Record Office, 1494-1509, Volume 2, Henry VII. His Majesty's Stationery Office (1916).

Cambridge, Corpus Christi College, MS 119: Letters Principally of Foreign Reformers, letter 21, [https://exhibits.stanford.edu/parker/catalog/xs417vg0804].

Cassell, John (1876) *Picturesque Europe: The British Isles*, 1st ed. Cassell, Petter, Galpin & Co.

Catalogue of Ancient Deeds, ed. H C Maxwell Lyte. Her Majesty's Stationery Service (1890).

Cavendish, George (1827) The Life of Cardinal Wolsey, 2nd ed. Harding & Lepard.

Cavendish, George (1825) The Life of Cardinal Wolsey and Metrical Visions, Volume II, ed. Samuel Weller Singer. Harding, Triphook & Lepard.

Cherry, Clare and Ridgway, Claire (2014) *George Boleyn: Tudor Poet, Courtier & Diplomat.* MadeGlobal Publishing.

Coope, Rosalys (1986) 'The 'Long Gallery': Its Origins, Development, Use, and Decoration', Architectural History, Vol. 29, pp. 43-67.

Dean, William.H. (1987) *Sir Thomas Boleyn: The courtier diplomat, 1477-1539*, [Doctoral thesis, West Virginia University].

Dillard, Adrienne (2017) *The Raven's Widow: A Novel of Jane Boleyn*. MadeGlobal Publishing.

Emery, Anthony (2006) *Greater Medieval Houses of England and Wales 1300-1500*, Vol III, 1st ed. Cambridge University Press.

Exchequer: King's Remembrancer: Escheators' Files, Inquisitions Post Mortem, Series II, and other Inquisitions, Henry VII to Elizabeth I, National Archives.

Fenton, Charlie (2021) *Jane Parker: The Downfall of Two Tudor Queens?* Chronos Books.

Foxe, John (1851) *Fox's Book of Martyrs: The Acts and Monuments of the Church*, Volume 3. G. Virtue.

Fox, Julia (2007) *Jane Boleyn: The Infamous Lady Rochford*. Phoenix.

Friedmann, Paul (1884) *Anne Boleyn: A Chapter of English History 1527-1536*, Volume I. Macmillan and Co.

Goodall, John (2011) *The English Castle*. Yale Books.

Goodhall, John (2014, 23 July) 'A Celebrity Castle, Hever Castle Kent part 1', *County Life*, pp. 46-50.

Gregory, Philippa (2003) *The Other Boleyn Girl*. Scribner.

Grosvenor, Bendor (2011, 15 December), 'Anne Boleyn regains her head', Art History News.
https://www.arthistorynews.com/articles/894_Anne_Boleyn_regains_her_head

Hall, Edward (1809) *Hall's chronicle: containing the history of England, during the reign of Henry the Fourth, and the succeeding monarchs, to the end of the reign of Henry the Eighth, in which are particularly described the manners and customs of those periods*. J Johnson.

The Harleian miscellany: or, A collection of scarce, curious, and entertaining pamphlets and tracts, as well in manuscript as in print (1744), Volume III. T. Osborne.

Harpsfield, Nicholas (1878) *A Treatise on the Pretended Divorce between Henry VIII and Catharine of Aragon*. Camden Society.

Historical Portraits Image Library, Philip Mould Ltd. http://www.historicalportraits.com/

Hodgson, John and F. C. Laird (1813) *The Beauties of England and Wales, or, Original Delineations, topographical, historical, and descriptive, of each county*, Volume XII: Part I. J. Harris.

Ireland, Samuel (1793) *Picturesque Views on the River Medway*, 1st ed. T. and J. Edgerton.

Ives, Eric (2004) *The life and death of Anne Boleyn*. Blackwell Publishing.

Knight, Charles (1850) *The Land We Live In: A Pictorial and Literary Sketch-book of the British Empire*, Volume III. Charles Knight.

Lelandi, Joannis (1770), *Antiquarii de Rebus Britannicis Collectanea*, Volume IV. Gul. & Jo. Richardson.

Letters and Papers, Foreign and Domestic, Henry VIII, ed. J S Brewer (London, 1920). These can be viewed online at https://www.british-history.ac.uk/search/series/letters-papers-hen8

Lindsey, Karen (1996) *Divorced, Beheaded, Survived: A Feminist Reinterpretation Of The Wives Of Henry VIII*. Da Capo Press.

Longueville, Olivia (2020, 4 December) 'Anne Boleyn's Education and Life at the French Court', https://olivialongueville.com/anne-boleyns-education-and-life-at-the-french-court/.

Mackay, Lauren (2018) *Among the Wolves of Court: The Untold Story of Thomas and George Boleyn*, 1st ed. I.B. Taurus.

Mantel, Hilary (2010) *Wolf Hall*. Picador.

The manuscripts of His Grace the Duke of Rutland: preserved at Belvoir Castle, Volume I, (HMSO, 1888).

Morris, Sarah, and Grueninger, Natalie (2013) *In the Footsteps of Anne Boleyn.* Amberley Publishing.

Mould, Philip, *'Portrait of Prince Arthur of Wales, c.1500'*, Historical Portraits Image Library, http://www.historicalportraits.com/Gallery.asp?Page=Item&ItemID=21

Morant, Philip (1763) *The History and Antiquities of the County of Essex*, Volume II. London.

Newman, John & Nikolaus Pevsner (2012) *Kent: West and the Weald*, 1st ed. Yale University Press.

Paget, Hugh (1981, November) 'The Youth of Anne Boleyn', Bulletin of the Institute of Historical Research, Volume 54, Issue 130, pp. 162–170.

Parsons, Rev. Canon W. L. E. (1935) 'Some Notes on the Boleyn Family', Norfolk Archaeology or Miscellaneous Tracts Relating to the Antiquities of the County of Norfolk
(Norfolk and Norwich Archaeological Society, 1935), XXV: pp. 386-407.

The Paston Letters, A.D. 1422-1509, ed. James Gairdner, Vol II, (Chatto & Windus, 1904).

Powlett, Catherine Lucy Wilhelmina Stanhope, Duchess of Cleveland (1889) *The Battle Abbey Roll with Some Account of the Norman Lineages, in Three Volumes*, Volume 1. John Murray.

Queen Victoria's Journals, Volume: 5 (20th May 1834 - 4th November 1834), http://www.queenvictoriasjournals.org/.

Royal Collection Trust, Scene from Anna Bolena c. 1837 - c. 1841, https://www.rct.uk/collection/980019-am; Anne Boleyn Clock 1530-1870?, https://www.rct.uk/collection/search#/4/collection/30018/anne-boleyn-clock

Rumens, Carol (2009, 10 August) 'Poem of the week: Whoso List to Hunt by Thomas Wyatt', *The Guardian*. https://www.theguardian.com/books/booksblog/2009/aug/10/poem-of-the-week-thomas-wyatt.

Russo, Stephanie (2020) *The Afterlife of Anne Boleyn: Representations of Anne Boleyn in Fiction and on the Screen*, 1st ed. Palgrave Macmillan.

Starkey, David, 'Henry VIII: The First Brexiteer', talk at the Festival Theatre, Hever Castle, 8 August 2018.

Starkey, D. R. (1974) 'The King's Privy Chamber 1485-1547', [Doctoral thesis, University of Cambridge].

Strype, John (1822) *Ecclesiastical memorials relating chiefly to religion and the reformation of it, and the emergencies of the Church of England, under King Henry VIII, King Edward VI and Queen Mary the First*, Volume I, Part I. Clarendon Press.

Thiemann, A, 'Anne of Cleves: The Queen of the Lower Rhine', Unpublished Thesis, Hever Castle Archives.

Toulman Smith, Lucy (1908) ed. *The Itinerary of John Leland*, Volume II, 1st ed. George Bell and Sons.

Wedgewood, Josiah. C. (1936) *History of Parliament: Biographies of The Members of The Commons House 1439-1509*. His Majesty's Stationery Office.

Weir, Alison (2015, 23 May) 'Is this Anne of Cleves?', https://tudortimes.co.uk/people/is-this-anne-of-cleves.

Wood, Mary Anne Everett (1846) ed. *Letters of royal and illustrious ladies of Great Britain, from the commencement of the twelfth century to the close of the reign of Queen Mary*, Volume II. Henry Colburn.

Wriothesley, Charles (1875) *A chronicle of England during the reigns of the Tudors, from A.D. 1485 to 1559*, Volume I. Camden Society.

Wynkyn de Worde, *The Maner of the Tryumphe of Caleys and Bulleyn: And The Noble Tryumphaunt Coronacyon of Quene Anne, Wyfe Unto the Most Noble Kynge Henry VIII, printed by Wynkyn de Worde, 1532-33*, edited by Edmund Goldsmid, Edinburgh, 1885.

Other books by Claire Ridgway

The Anne Boleyn Collection:
The Real Truth About the Tudors

The Anne Boleyn Collection II:
Anne Boleyn and the Boleyn Family

The Anne Boleyn Collection III:
Celebrating Ten Years of TheAnneBoleynFiles

The Fall of Anne Boleyn:
A Countdown

George Boleyn:
Tudor Poet, Courtier & Diplomat (with Clare Cherry)

Illustrated Kings and Queens of England

Tudor Places of Great Britain

Sweating Sickness: In a Nutshell

On this Day in Tudor History

The Life of Anne Boleyn Colouring Book

CPSIA information can be obtained
at www.ICGtesting.com
Printed in the USA
LVHW051947160721
692488LV00005B/7